Center Dock
A True Story

by
Steve Walton

authorHOUSE®

AuthorHouse™
1663 Liberty Drive, Suite 200
Bloomington, IN 47403
www.authorhouse.com
Phone: 1-800-839-8640

© 2008 Steve Walton. All rights reserved.

No part of this book may be reproduced, stored in a retrieval system, or transmitted by any means without the written permission of the author.

First published by AuthorHouse   7/11/2008

ISBN: 978-1-4343-9265-7 (sc)

Printed in the United States of America
Bloomington, Indiana

This book is printed on acid-free paper.

Dedication

This book is dedicated to the memory of Mr. and Mrs. Carl Pfafflin and all Pfafflin Lake lifeguards, wherever you are.

Acknowledgments

I'm indebted to Sherilyn Walton for her editorial work, and Danny Miller for providing information and to my younger brother Tom for keeping me honest in describing the events depicted in this book.

Foreword

From a rural lake in southern Indiana to a bridge in Pompano Beach Florida, Walton transcends the normal realm of humor by taking us on a roller coaster ride of emotions and side splitting laughter. Spanning the years from 1960 to 1965, he relates his experiences as a summer lifeguard at Pfafflin Lake in Newburgh, Indiana, while attending what is now the University of Evansville. Being continually bested in swimming feats, humbled by women, attacked by bees, and nearly expelled from college, he strives to understand the complexities of life, while maintaining his dignity and some semblance of respectability.

Notes

The events depicted in this book are true, although the exact timing of the events may be inaccurate. I'm not really sure of the exact number of years I worked at the lake, but for the purpose of continuity and readability I used a four year period. To those persons mentioned in this book who feel negatively impacted by it, I apologize, as that was not my intent.

Introduction

FOR SOME REASON, or several reasons, Bob Dodge failed to negotiate the curve just past the Knob Hill Inn in Newburgh, Indiana, that early morning. That incident, though traumatic for Bob, for me, set the stage for an adventure that lasted several years and which still remains with me to this day.

Newburgh, Indiana, is a small village eight miles east of Evansville on the Ohio River in southern Indiana. Two miles east of Newburgh is a man-made lake which today is still known as Pfafflin Lake. The lake was a primary summer attraction for the student crowd, families, and adventurous souls seeking a day of cool water, fishing, boating and beer drinking.

Often, I would accompany my older brother and his high school football teammates, as they and their sailor cap-turned-downward clad girl friends embarked on a day of fun and fried chicken. I was seven years old then. Family gatherings at the lake were especially prized occurrences involving long picnic tables, cousins, friends, stories of the War and The Great Depression and humoring the family's favorite priest.

Our favorite padre was Father Urban Knapp, who never hesitated to enjoy a home cooked meal or the comfort of fine cigars. He also enjoyed swimming and was a master of the freestyle crawl stroke. My dad and Father Urban coached football together at Saint Benedict's Elementary School in Evansville during the 40s. On many a Sunday afternoon, Father Urban instilled within me the fundamentals of the crawl stroke. I've never forgotten what he taught me about swimming, and even to this day still think of him every morning when I hit the pool for my lap routine.

The most fun day of my life was my elementary school eighth grade graduation party at the lake, which culminated in a giant battle between the sexes. The girls were in one rubber boat, boys in the other. I'm unsure as to what the objective was, but we proceeded to dispel eight years of peer induced frustration, hidden angers, pent-up jealousies, petty rivalries and God only knows what else. No high seas pirate attack could match the violence directed toward each other that day. We attacked them, they attacked us, we attacked each other. It was the highlight of my early school days.

Pfafflin Lake was not always a lake. The area at one time was a huge apple orchid, and for many years after the lake was dug out, apple trees were still in abundance and continued to produce. The lake was comprised of three areas: fishing, swimming and boating. It was huge. The surrounding grounds presented an ideal place for picnicking, walking, and any other outdoor activity so desired.

There were two swimming areas. The south beach, as I always referred to it, had about a ten yard swath of sand with the grass beach behind it leading up to a bath house. The north beach was much larger with a similar layout. However, behind the grassy beach area on the north beach was a grassy hill area which eventually became known as beer hill. It was in this area where alcohol was permitted and needless to say led to most of the problems for Carl Pfafflin.

I don't remember Carl Pfafflin as a youngster. However this gentleman and his family came to play an enormous role in my life and I still grieve today over his passing. As my lifeguarding summers began, I came to admire and love this man as a son loves his father. He was older then, and projected an image as a gruff, suntanned farmer, stubborn to the core, fiercely independent and handy with a shotgun.

He wasn't too diplomatic with troublemakers and often displayed his disdain by yelling over his loud speaker at errant swimmers and other violators of lake rules. But beneath his leather exterior, was a gentle, kind and peaceful man of uncompromising integrity, sincerity and character. He owned it all and managed it with an iron fist. He was one of my heroes.

I began working at the lake as a lifeguard during my senior year in high school. It felt as if I were entering a new realm of reality, one which I grew to love and cherish even to this day. It was the decade of the sixties, and John Kennedy's new frontier. It was a time of war and of the Peace Corps. It was a time of change.

So let us begin

Invitation to the Dance

IT WAS 1960, and I was four months from graduating from Memorial High School in Evansville. Four years of frustration were at an end, and my college years were about to begin. I chose Evansville College primarily due to its rising star in the basketball world. It was also affordable and in walking distance from home. Even before graduation, parental pressure regarding summer employment began to be applied in small, yet unrelenting doses.

My mother was well known in local Evansville political circles having served as one of former Evansville mayor Vance Hartke's precinct committee persons. Along with a new basketball stadium to house the rising tide of the college's basketball program, the city council also voted to build a public outdoor swimming facility named after Mayor Hartke.

Needless to say, I was told that strings could be pulled, and should I desire to become a lifeguard at Hartke Pool, that I was in. All I had to do was get my lifesaving certificate. I found this option extremely intriguing, much more so than bagging groceries or mowing lawns.

In May the YMCA in Evansville was offering a lifesaving class. I enrolled and began to put into practice the swimming skills taught to me years earlier by Father Urban. I loved it and committed myself to become a strong swimmer and to perhaps increase my social standing with the ladies. Well, one out of two wasn't bad.

While in that class, I met a short, stocky, crew cut guy who as I later found out was honing his lifeguarding skills for his summer job at Pfafflin Lake.

Danny Miller was a few years older than I. His father owned Miller Bakery in downtown Evansville across from the A&P. My dad often stopped in his store on his way to or from work to buy pastries. After learning of my intent to work at Hartke Pool, Danny mentioned there may be an opening at Pfafflin Lake due to losing a guard through an auto accident. (Bob Dodge). I was elated! Could this really be happening?

A week after the lifesaving class ended, I was invited to the lake for a test swim. I was fully aware of my swimming weaknesses. I could barely swim the Red Cross required quarter mile for lifesaving certification without changing strokes. Although the endurance was there from playing grade school and high school football, my leg muscles were experiencing a totally different environment. My thoughts kept drifting back to bags of groceries and six inch high lawns. I had to give this a try.

Mr Pfafflin told me to swim out to the center of the lake and back as fast as I could without stopping. It felt as though I was pulling two tons of flab as I put everything I had into those strokes. Less than half way out, my leg muscles decided to go on strike. I was beginning to hurt. Bagging groceries began to seem attractive once again. But no, I was not going to give in. I forged ahead in moderate distress, made the turn and kicked in for the stretch run. I knew I looked bad, but kept going thinking that I had at least tried. I was convinced that my career at the lake had ended before it had started, and that Father Urban would disavow any responsibility or knowledge of my actions.

I came out of the water, dried off and prepared for the judgment. Mr Pfafflin said he liked my upper body strength and endurance and that I was hired. I thought to myself they must truly be desperate. I've been celebrating ever since. I started two days later.

A quick dash off to Beards Sporting Goods netted me two whistles with plastic straps, two pair of nerdy looking swim trunks, an orange cap and a large beach towel. I was ready.

Even though I had been to the lake countless times as a youth, I was still not fully aware of the vastness of the property. On my first day I arrived at the lake early and decided to take a long walk around the entire perimeter of the grounds. I had never been to the north side of the lake up to that time. The entire acreage sloped gently toward the lake. Picnic tables were everywhere. Apples were beginning to appear on the trees. It felt great to be away from the strains and discipline of the classroom and harsh days of winter. I was free. To me this was hallowed ground. I encircled the entire property and mentally adopted it as my own.

Although I qualified as a city boy, I felt more at home at the lake than anywhere else. It was all country and I loved it. Today I think back to that walk and now know what Billy Crystal felt like riding off on that horse in the movie "City Slickers." As I traversed around the back end of the property, I felt exulted as if in a wilderness alone. This was my new world. My cup was no longer half empty, but half full and getting more fuller.

I gave no thought to the manner of transportation. Until I was able to carpool with somebody, my parents had to drive me back and forth to the lake each day. So I quickly formulated a plan, which involved me doing nothing and netting me a set of wheels. All I had to do was wait.

My plan worked. After only two days of parental taxi service, my dad approached me and said, "Let's go." I picked out what I thought was a decent set of wheels. Delivery would be the following afternoon. My dad took possession and drove the car up to the lake that afternoon.

I was set! I nick named the car Blue-Boy due to its bluish-green color. A year later, it would be renamed, not by me, but by the actions of my mother. More on that event later.

The swimming area had two docks. The front dock was close to the south beach and had two slides and a couple of low diving boards, a medium board, and one high dive platform. The water was generally shallow in the front of the dock, and it was in this area where the little kids would do their thing. There were three guard stands on the beach and two standing positions on the dock. On busy weekend days, all five positions were manned. On my first day, I was assigned the middle beach position.

The big moment had arrived. I climbed up, sat down, took a deep breath, said a prayer, and promptly got stung by a bee. I wondered at that point whether Hartke Pool had bees and if I had made a mistake. I began to formulate long term goals while sitting on my wooden throne. I knew I wasn't the fastest or strongest swimmer, so I endeavored to become the best set of eyes. I guarded those kids like an eagle and swam on every break and consumed at least three Payday candy bars and five Pepsi colas a day. I also began to get a tan. But my biggest goal was to someday be assigned to the center dock.

The center dock was for the big boys, three swings, two diving boards, and a twenty seven foot diving platform, all surrounded by twenty foot deep water. It set in the middle of the lake and required a long swim just to reach it. It was this swim that resulted in a lot of our rescues. This was not for kiddies, this was the big time.

There were two guard posts on the center dock. Someday, I hoped to occupy one of them. Until then I bided my time. I swam when I could, watched the girls and began to build a reputation for having eagle eyes. I was so dedicated that I would come to the lake on my days off and swim and frolic about on the center dock.

Invitation to the Dance

The center dock always scared me. I often visualized someone going off one of the swings and letting loose too early, or not letting loose at all and smashing into the edge of the dock never to be seen again. The twenty-seven foot diving platform was the real killer. If you landed wrong, or failed to protect certain parts of your anatomy, it could be disastrous and was on many occasions. I had never gone off that platform, but was destined to overcome my fear and prove whatever it was I was trying to prove. Finally, on a hot Wednesday in June, I climbed to the top.

I was always taught that the best way to overcome fear was to meet it head-on and attack. Not only was I going to attack, I was going to do it headfirst. I hit the water at a decent angle, feeling exhilarated, I slowly rose to the surface experiencing both relief and an unusually cold sensation in my groin area. It took nine minutes to find my swimming trunks. I made the guard on the center dock swear to secrecy under penalty of being made to swallow sun tan oil. Next time, I would be better prepared.

After that incident I ensured my trunks were sufficiently tightened in the right places and vowed to wear extra protection during future high dive deeds of daring.

For many years, the twenty-seven footer had been the scene of unparalleled drama. It witnessed courage, disaster, triumph, pain, and the onslaught of the 101st Airborne from Fort Campbell, Kentucky. On most Sunday afternoons, these screaming eagles would use the high dives as if they were gliders in the Normandy Invasion.

Ascending to the top, usually in groups of about fifteen, they would practice their jumping techniques in view of an astonished and mesmerized audience…STAND UP, HOOK UP, CHECK EQUIPMENT, SOUND OFF, STAND BY THE DOOR. As the lone jump master would cast a final eye over the edge, then yell-GO, all fifteen would hurl themselves into the twenty foot abyss, one at a time. How they each hit the water instead of each other still mystifies me today. Certain that not all would surface, the guards stood ready and tense knowing that action was imminent. How they all survived was a miracle.

Not to be outdone by the guys, some strong minded females sometimes dared to test fate and perform the leap into oblivion. Most were ill equipped for the feat, but not as ill equipped as their bikinis. Many times they would hit the water, and soon a head would surface along with two floating bikini bra cups. I welcomed them into my secret high dive stripper club.

As the summer passed and I gained experience in the fine art of lifeguarding, I developed several swimmer watching techniques. Although certainly not original, I nevertheless began to use these methods more and more especially during the busy days. I found that with fifteen swimmers or less that head counting was somewhat effective. After a quick head count, and adding and subtracting the entries and exits from the water, it was easy to keep track of the numbers. This worked until the monotony set in; lost count, or became distracted by bikinis or other nearby beach area phenomena.

Scanning was effective for large crowds. With this method my eyes continually scanned large areas looking for jerky movements or unusual movement. For me, keeping the eyes moving was the key, especially when a lot of kiddies were near the shore. The major drawback in this case was it induced fatigue, and, as I learned later in life, heavy doses of eye strain.

Today, modern managers call it "outside the box" or sometimes "situational awareness." Watching an assigned area is good, concentration is essential, however, combining those elements with the ability to think and reason, in my opinion, is an unbeatable combination. For example, if a boat is passing through the swimming area, then it is logical that if someone is on a nearby diving board and swing, the potential for conflict is increased, requiring attention. If there is a group of divers on the high dive platform, then the element of peer pressure usually becomes a factor, often resulting in a hurried dive, or attempts to exceed one's abilities. This method would come into play in a near tragic event three years later.

Successful conclusions of long distance swimmers attempting to make it across the lake or to the center dock could easily be evaluated by observing their swimming technique. With the crawl stroke, if the arms were not coming out the water completely in the reach, or the head and upper body rotated excessively from side to side, that indicated potential weakness. Another danger signal would be if they simply stopped. One of three things would then occur; they would either start up again, sink, or begin to flail. In either case the guard was already on the way.

I never used a deep water rescue to embarrass the victim. If someone were struggling to make it across the lake, often, depending on the depth of their problem, a mere push or word of encouragement resulted in the individual striking off to a successful conclusion. If weakness in a swimmer was detected early enough, it was possible to slowly make your way out unnoticed and be within a few feet of the individual without his knowledge.

On many occasions, a struggling swimmer was escorted across the lake without his knowledge. One day, while on a break, I started across the lake just in back of a young boy who was about ten yards in front of me. I was proceeding slowly on a breast stroke when I sensed he was beginning to tire. I swam up to him, and using psychology, told him I was tired, and asked if I could hold on to his shoulder for a minute. We both rested a bit, him thinking he was helping me, when I was actually supporting him. After about thirty seconds, we took off and upon reaching the beach, I gasped and thanked him for helping me across. Ten minutes later, he took off again in the opposite direction and without hesitation made it across with renewed vigor and confidence. I had won one for the Gipper.

For many years, Mr. Pfafflin had been concerned about leakage through the lake dam. It seemed the lake had been populated by a family of muskrats, and other potential leak generating critters. When the lake had been dug out, the eastern edge had to be raised to hold the water. Dirt had been scooped out from behind the area similar to a river levee. The ensuing change in landscape became known as the dam. There was a footpath on top connecting the north and south beaches. We had a rainy week that June, and one slow weekday afternoon, we were tasked with digging trenches on the slope of the dam so as to capture the perceived flow of leaking water. I think the intent was to keep the leakage contained so as to not erode the entire area. We worked on this project for about two weeks. Each day the boss would carefully inspect the phantom leakage convinced that disaster was imminent.

I was shocked that this fear still existed years after Mr Pfafflin's death. After the lake had closed in 1967, Mildred Pfafflin , the daughter, had moved into the new Pfafflin house. One day, I paid her a visit and related my intention of possibly living on the lake. She was flabbergasted. She said it was dangerous down there and that she felt sorry for the people living near the lake. I couldn't believe my ears. I asked her what the problem was. She answered that she was certain the dam was going to let go.

She also indicated her intent to sell the house and move to Hot Springs, Arkansas. She said that was primarily due to her belief that Highway 662 was also going to collapse into the Ohio River.

Pfafflin Lake was situated just off Highway 662 which bordered on the edge of the Ohio River. Each rainy year, a portion of the road would sometimes erode requiring substantial restructuring and bracing. But in no way was that road then or now in danger of collapsing. Mildred felt differently. I hope she found Ozark heaven.

The Name Game

I THOUGHT STEVE DUNCAN was the best swimmer we had, but he tended to lollygag too much and not watch the water. He lived in Evansville, so we commuted together on days when we worked the same shift. We became good pals. He had ambitions of becoming a corporate lawyer. He had huge hands and used them to his advantage when swimming. I could never match his speed, even though he was much taller, and heavier than I. I was more stocky and compact in build and therefore believed less effected by water resistance. I later learned this theory was completely wrong.

Steve Knienabor was also a good swimmer but he tended to use the scissors kick when he swam the crawl stroke. I think he could have been a lot better using the standard kick. Steve K was a nice sort of guy who appeared to me to be somewhat aloof. I liked him though, but felt that he didn't care for me much. Both Steves and Danny Miller were excellent volleyball players.

John Steele was a wiry, yet strong swimmer who was always concerned about his physique. I remember one day one of the guys had brought a set of weights to the lake, and John would spent all of his break time lifting weights on the island. This went on for hours. After each repetition of lifting, Bob would examine himself carefully in the reflection of the juke box convinced that differences were beginning to show. He left that day feeling as though his body had changed for the better. We should all have been so lucky to have experienced such a rapid transformation.

Phil Smith was the youngest, still in high school when he started. He evolved into a good swimmer and a superb diver. Phil was unmatched on the three meter board.

Danny Miller was the top dog at that time. He was the veteran, having worked at the lake since 1955. A tremendous swimmer, he could swim the crawl forever without turning his head, a distinct advantage in lifeguarding. Danny was king of the center dock, our rock, and my mentor.

Those are the guys I remember. There were several others whose names I can't recall, and several part time weekenders. We were diverse, yet, had a lot in common, and for the most part got along fairly well. I do remember two of our part-timers who later came on full-time, Tom Farrell and Charlie Brenner.

There were two other lake inhabitants who served as, for lack of better definition, the lake mascots. Jeff and Cindy Barnes were the pre-teen children of John and Mildred Barnes. Mildred, as mentioned earlier, was the daughter of Mr Pfafflin and handled most of the concessionary operations at the lake.

These two kids were like miniature hurricanes who took advantage of every possible hour of every day to explore the wonders of their water world. It was Cindy who said I reminded her of a TV character named Uncle Wally. Well, the name stuck and I was forever known as Uncle Wally. I suspect very few people at the lake ever came to know my real name. Jeff and Cindy were complete opposites. Jeff was thin, mild mannered who loved baseball, especially Sandy Koufax.

I sold Jeff his first guitar, and the last I heard, had become an accomplished musician. His water specialty was diving to the bottom of the lake searching for rare antiques. One time he came up with a pair of bikini bottoms. This event created quite a stir and needless to say left many wondering how such a loss could occur without obvious ramifications being noticed, one of the enduring mysteries of Pfafflin Lake.

Cindy, on the other hand, was a stocky muscular specimen of unbridled energy who in a lot of ways reminded me of a bulldog. I enjoyed her antics and practical jokes. She loved to dive, but never seemed to be able to get her legs straight. Her favorite water specialty was the center dock swings; no one was better than Cindy on the swings. She had this unusual technique of throwing the swing back to its starting point as she let go. A trick I never mastered.

My real name took another nose dive thanks to the well meaning efforts of a certain Mrs. Gardner.

Mrs. Gardner was the ticket taker at the entry point for the lake. She spent her golden years housed in a small ticket taker sort of building no larger than a modern day theater ticket booth. Mrs. Gardner was one of my favorite characters. I enjoyed talking to her when I arrived for work. Upon learning my last name was Walton, she told of a past relative named John Walton. From that day forward, she always referred to me as John. Thus was formulated my second Pfafflin Lake name. I arrived at the gate as John, and arrived at the lake as Uncle Wally.

As the years passed, I became more convinced that Mrs. Gardner actually believed I was the reincarnation of her great uncle. Whether due to senility, senior moments, or harboring a deeply hidden sense of humor on her part, I continue to wonder what her real thoughts were on the matter. In any case, I was often late for work due to the intriguing conversations Mrs. Gardner and I shared on everything from Newburgh history to the golden age of the Pfafflin apple orchards.

Having been raised in a strict parochial school environment characterized by ruler wielding nuns to fist wielding Holy Cross brothers, I was beginning to sense that this job was a door opening to the other side of the world. I began to see and experience a wider spectrum of society. I came to realize that not everyone went to church on Sunday, not everyone used the same vocabulary, and not everyone came from the same socio-economic environment. I had never seen anyone really drunk before. I had never seen a real snake in its natural setting, nor had I ever seen up close the beauty of a well executed high dive. I was awakening to the wonders of the world, and I relished it all.

That first year at the lake was like being in high school without having to go to class. I made a lot of friends, learned to work with all kinds of personalities, which helped me immensely in later years in the military when I had to work with morons. I improved my social skills which I needed badly, and was exposed to a wide array of lovely ladies. I was still somewhat of an introverted loner and felt I was beginning to emerge from my parochial shell. This experience was what I needed, and I intended to make the most of it; most important, I was happy, and I was Uncle Wally.

The summer passed without a lot of fanfare. I fell into the lake routine quickly and became confident that this job was a calling. I kept remembering the many hours I spent as a kid doing what the kids were doing in front of me now, on the same dock, in the same manner, yelling the same things. I couldn't believe that the posts sticking out of the lake were still there. Those posts in the early days were used to moor the rubber boats. A boat dock had been put in later but those same posts brought back memories of Father Urban making me swim out to the post and back without touching. Even the taste of the water was the same since my childhood days. I will always remember that taste. The trees were much larger, and the guard shack had been moved from a perch over the water to further up the beach.

The Pfafflin main residence was located on the main entry road behind a giant oak tree just as the road sloped toward the parking area.

It had a neat little circular drive and offered views of th
as well as a large portion of the lake. It was a perfect co
surrounded by trees and lush lawns.

The south portion of the Pfafflin property bordered on a farm owned by the Morton family. Mr. Morton raised horses and often his horses would hang out by the fence on the south beach to be entertained and occasionally fed by the beach crowds.

I'm not sure what was beyond the western boundary of the property, except somewhere in those woods was a secret entrance offering free access to the lake as long as you didn't get caught. Mr. Pfafflin had a unique way of dealing with those youngsters who dared the deed. He would allow them to come in thinking that they had not been spotted. After they had settled in to their spot and commenced their activity, Mr. Pfafflin would approach them with an offer they couldn't refuse.

He would tell them they were trespassing, and had a choice of either facing a $100 fine and three days in jail or call their parents to come and pick them up. The latter choice was always selected, as was his intent. Any serious violators of rules such as fighting, disobeying the guards, or constantly throwing sand would result in a phone call to parents. Older violators faced the wrath of the County Sheriff. The Newburgh jail was usually full on Sunday evenings.

Another technique used to sneak onto the grounds involved the old tried and true method of hiding in the trunk of a friend's car. This worked sometimes, but more often than not, these hidden bandits were doomed even before reaching the entry point. It seemed these trunk tyrants would stop along the highway just prior to entering the drive, and proceed in front of other arriving patrons, to perform the disappearing ritual, not realizing these other honest patrons would rat them out. Mrs. Gardner would be told of the pending ruse and after writing down the license plate, would tell them to either open the trunk, or be prepared to open their pocketbooks for the Sheriff.

Family Shenanigans

ALL THROUGH ELEMENTARY SCHOOL and high school I would accompany my parents and my little brother on their annual pilgrimage to Daytona Beach, Florida. These trips had a profound impact on my personality, and contributed toward my undying love of the water. I had always loved the ocean and would spend most of those days taking on the waves while avoiding jelly fish stings. I loved to sit and watch the lifeguards as they sat in those huge wooden stands. I often fantasized about becoming a beach bum and living in some shack near the beach, or even becoming a surf guard. These trips made me begin to ponder my future. It was during these treks that I came to really love and respect the water, and knew then that somehow I was not finished with any of it. I actually contemplated swimming the English Channel someday; I was suffering from visions of grandeur.

I would swim in the ocean during the day, and then we would all sit outside by the hotel pool at night eating pizza, and watching the moon make its appearance on the ocean horizon. Yes, I knew that environment would somehow find its way into my life again.

Center Dock

Some of those family excursions to Florida generated high drama. We experienced the many normal aspects of vacation bliss after arriving at our destinations. The nightmares occurred in our attempts to get to our destination.

One year, during May, when I was in the seventh grade, we took off for a week of sunshine and oysters at beautiful Daytona Beach. My dad had recently acquired a new set of false teeth.

It was customary at that time that when families went on extended vacations, keys to the house would be left with a neighbor. We left about 1:00 am in order to avoid heavy traffic on Highway 41. We had dropped the keys to our house in the neighbor's door slot mail box. All was well. Not much conversation had taken place. I was attempting to sleep; my mother was knitting. After about two hours we were in central Kentucky when my dad started whistling. Suddenly, he pulls to the side of the road, yells "3$*)@& I forgot my teeth!" Back we went.

We arrived back home around 4:45am unable to get into the house. We had to break into our own house. I was aware that one of the back basement windows might offer the best means of entry, since I would often shoot my BB gun from that window at birds gathering in our backyard cherry tree. The window was locked but with a little bit of shoulder pressure the latch broke off and in I went to retrieve my dad's set of chompers.

We braced the window up as best we could and once again proceeded out of our driveway confident that the whole episode had gone unnoticed. We again drove down our street and turned onto Lincoln Avenue heading for Highway 41. Two blocks from the highway we saw two cop cars with lights flashing coming the opposite direction and turning down our street. My dad let out with a few more obscenities, and finally said, "To hell with it, let's go to Florida!" The early morning drama was not yet over.

It was a beautiful sunrise as we approached the Tennessee border. Just as thoughts of breakfast began to occupy our minds, my dad suddenly swerved to the right and hitting something in the road.

Normally, skunk smells diminish after an hour or so, but this time the smell remained and seemed to be getting worse. After just reaching the Georgia line, my mother was gagging and demanding we stop to investigate the source of this nasal discomfort. We pulled into a service station and requested our car be put on a jack for a peek underneath.

My dad told the attendant that he thought we had hit a skunk, but that something wasn't right. Up went the car, and to everyone's dismay, the skunk, or what remained of one, was lodged between the engine block and fender well. It took an enormous amount of cash to persuade the attendant to bring forth the hoses and relieve us of this uninvited guest.

It would not be my last experience with a skunk.

As I recall, I was a sophomore in high school when it was decided to spend the week before Christmas in Florida, then drive up to spend the holidays with my older brother who was then stationed in the Air Force in Selma, Alabama. We stayed in Fort Lauderdale that year, and decided to drive across the Everglades to the Gulf coast, and then up into Alabama. That decision would haunt my parents until their death.

Christmas was on a Monday that year, and our objective was to arrive in Selma on Christmas Eve day. We left Lauderdale on Friday and headed along the secluded Everglades highway toward the little town of Everglades City. It was about 4:00 pm and we were about fifteen miles north of Everglades City, Florida, when the engine heat warning light went on in the car. Soon, steam was pouring from the radiator. We pulled into a service station. The attendant suggested we flush the cooling system. We ate a quick snack while fresh coolant was poured into our radiator.

It felt good to be rid of the problem, and off we went. Five miles from Everglades City, the engine heat warning light came on again, with steam once again pouring out. We turned off the main road and made it into a garage in Everglades City. The mechanic told us we needed a new thermostat, but it would have to be ordered and the earliest it would arrive was on the 26th, the day after Christmas.

We were so dismayed at this turn of events, we never thought to call and notify my brother of our pending tardiness. We checked into the Everglades Motel.

The small town of Everglades City, Florida at that time was nothing more than a small village. There was a service station, a post office, and a small grocery store. The town-folk evidently had closed everything up for the holidays. After checking into the motel, we were told we were the only tenants and that the staff of two people were leaving for the holidays and that the motel would be closed, and when we left, to just leave the key on one of the beds. Little did we know that with their departure, we were not able to call out on the phone-primarily because the motel had no phone service. We were stranded, and the only food we had was a box of stale fig-bars.

There we sat for four days. Christmas came and went. We ate the fig bars and took many strolls around scenic Everglades City Florida. My dad swore, my mother cried. We opened a few of the Christmas gifts we had brought.

Finally around noon on the 26th, the mechanic came over to tell us the car was ready. Again, not thinking to call my brother from the garage, we took off and finally arrived late in the afternoon of December 27th.

As we pulled onto his street we noticed a state police car in his driveway and one in front of his house. It seemed that a missing persons report had been filed with the state police. The Civil Air Patrol was conducting an air search, and the Coast Guard had been alerted. When we walked into the house, my brother was on the phone with the FBI. He never forgave us!

The Reckoning

I SPENT EACH AVAILABLE minute that summer improving my swimming skills. During the breaks, I would swim across the lake multiple times with an occasional body dive to the bottom. Two of my strength improving techniques involved pulling one of the small metal scooter boats across the lake and back. The second and most difficult feat was to sink one of the metal beach chairs to the bottom, then body dive and attempt to pull it to the surface. I rarely succeeded, especially in the deeper water. However, I felt I was getting much stronger. By midsummer, I was hard as a rock, tanned, and felt invincible. All I needed was a girl friend to watch the fireworks with among other things.

Every Fourth of July, we had a fireworks display. It tended to be the same setup each year culminating in a colorful display of the American flag. What was unique is that half of the fireworks were set off on the center dock necessitating high dives into the water after each firework was lit. Oh, what drama and adventure. I hoped to one day be one of those lucky lighters. My chance would come sooner than I thought.

As my first summer at the lake was ending, I experienced what I will refer to as a reckoning. The south beach bath house had two entries, one for men and one for women, with a small wall separating the two entries. Our lifeguard shack was near the east end of the beach and just off the sandy portion. A small window in the back afforded an unrestricted view of the female entry to the bath house.

It was late August, and almost dark when the two young ladies finally decided to leave. They were the last swimmers left, and I had worked the late shift and was the only guard remaining. I went to the guard shack and proceeded to change into my street clothes. I put away my equipment which consisted of a bottle of baby oil, a cap and a whistle. At this point, let me point out that neither the bath houses nor the guard shack had lights.

I very quickly dropped my swimming trunks and while standing there in my birthday suit I caught a glimpse of movement out the back window near the bath house. What to my wondering eyes did I see, but one of the ladies completely naked. Choosing not to go inside the bath house due to darkness, she elected to change clothes just behind the entry wall. I saw her, but she didn't see me. She had just slipped out of her swim suit and was standing there ringing it out. Her dark hair almost touched the ground as she bent over to slip on her shorts. In joyous thanks to God, I let it all sink in as she put on a halter. I knew at that moment I had found a second home and eternal bliss.

Sitting on a lifeguard stand offers one the opportunity for a close up look at reality. It is truly an education unto itself. That first year, I witnessed many aspects of human life. I began to see the effects of poverty and parental neglect. Kids were often left on their own at the lake for the entire day without money to buy food or drinks. I saw kids so overprotected by parents they were afraid to go into the water. On the other hand, I also witnessed the good side of human nature, well behaved kids being kids and having the time of their lives, laughing, swimming, diving and pretending the guards didn't know when they were peeing in the lake.

Sometimes it was humorous, but most of time I felt sorry for the unsuspecting souls who entered the water, then remained motionless. Woe to those who didn't keep moving. Little fish would nip at the smallest blemish on a person. I could always tell when it was coming. Into the water they would go, a slight hesitation, a startled jerk followed by a high pitched-squeal, and a quick retreat back onto the beach. Many made the mistake of believing that getting into deeper water would solve the problem. The fish would also go after belly buttons and certain anatomical parts found on the upper chests of men. These fish nips turned a lot of people against the lake and often complained to us as if it were our fault. I believe we lost a lot of family business due to our inability to control the fish population.

Nothing cleared a lake full of swimmers quicker than a SNAKE ALERT.

Down the center of the lake area was what we referred to as a tree line. This line of trees extended the entire length of the property, across the center of the lake and beyond. When the lake had been dug out, a portion of these trees had to be felled to accommodate the lake. This tree line, although only submerged stumps then, constituted the border between the fishing and swimming areas. The remaining trees on land were still there and constituted part of the landscape. Those trees provided ample shade, helped control water drainage and erosion, provided a perfect home for the annual migration of ducks, and a permanent home for snakes.

One particular area in the tree line on the north beach just behind the concession stand was often the scene of sudden outbursts of screaming and chaos, as the occasional snake would make its way to the water for a day of baby duck snacking and human harassment.

Center Dock

They were easy to spot. A small dark object protruding from the water and moving slowly, yet deliberately, followed by a perfectly uniform wake. The words "clear the water" often resulted in a few stares followed by a slow questioned withdraw from the water. However the words "clear the water-snake" would turn a somber, quiet, pristine country lake into an arena of screaming, thrashing, panicky humanity charging head-on up the beach, into their cars, up onto the laps of the guards and even out of the lake property entirely, rivaling a buffalo stampede, the Oklahoma Land Rush and The Charge of the Light Brigade all rolled into one.

One July afternoon, I feared for a kids' life as he chose to ignore the warning. It was nearly closing time, with just a few swimmers remaining. I spotted what looked like a snake entering into his vicinity just on the western edge of the swimming area and about twenty feet from the beach. I didn't want to make a big deal out of it, so I calmly walked to the edge of the water and asked him along with several others to exit the water, because of a possible snake threat. He was the only one remaining stating that he was not afraid of a little snake. I momentarily lost sight of what I thought had been a snake. He turned around and was about to head for the center dock when he felt a wet slithery sensation on his shoulder. This kid did not run from the water, he leapt from the water like a frog leaps lily pads, screaming in absolute horror.

I went out to examine the area and lo and behold I found that slithery culprit, grabbed it and presented it to the kid with my compliments. He and his mother were quite surprised at how that little tree twig resembled a snake. As I resumed my position on the chair, I overheard his mother saying, "Next time, you had better listen to the lifeguard."

Snakes, giant turtles, and the occasional fox never bothered Carl Pfafflin. It was muskrats that he waged war against.

He believed that these large aquatic creatures over the years had reigned havoc with the under-ground integrity of the lake and therefore had to be neutralized. I was well reminded of this fact, when one morning, having just donned my work togs, and about to exit the guard shack, I heard KABOOM-KABOOM just outside and to my right. I hit the floor believing that we were under attack from either the Viet Cong, or one of my former girl friends bent on extracting some sort of revenge. A quiet hush followed as I slowly opened the door expecting to meet death at any moment.

I peeked to the right and spotted Mr Pfafflin in a crouched position aiming his shotgun at the water. Suddenly, another volley, KABOOM-KABOOM, as the agitated water blossomed, and again flattened out, an ugly critter floated to the surface. He had nailed a muskrat. He proudly hoisted the remains of the critter from the water, content in the knowledge that a message had been sent to the muskrat crime syndicate.

My first year ended with most of my dignity intact. Although, seldom beating any of the other guys in small scale ad-hoc speed contests, I had gained the reputation of being a good all-around guard. I had become a much stronger swimmer and felt confident I would be re-hired the following year. I knew I had to work on my speed and leg kick. It was off to college for most of us. Although not aware of the off season swimming related plans of the others, I had planned on returning to the Y that winter for more lifesaving and water safety instructor certification.

Mondays with the NYF

I WAS WELL PREPARED for the second year. Having tried to satisfy my parents' desire for me to become a doctor or medical technician, I embarked on a pre-med curriculum during my first year of college. All went well until chemistry. I had trouble with it in high school and worse trouble with it in college. After two attempts with incompetent instructors and barely passing the course the second time, I resolved that the medical profession was not in my future. As a result of my experiences at the lake that first year, and mesmerized by the interactions of people, I decided to major in sociology.

By the May 1st opening day, I had honed my lifesaving skills, concentrating on deep water retrieval techniques, swimming speed, and had acquired my Red Cross instructor certificate. As I recall most of the same crew was back. The picnic tables were all freshly painted, the bathhouses clean as a bath house could be, concession stands filled to the brim, and the lake smell permeated the air-*oh how I loved the smell of lake in the morning, it smelled like victory!*

Those early May days passed in glorious normalcy. Some of the rescues were dramatic and serious. We took credit for a "save" when it was believed that the person would have drowned, or experienced a near death situation if we hadn't been there. I accumulated 11 saves within a two-hour period one Monday morning thanks to the Newburgh Youth Foundation.

The Newburgh Youth Foundation (NYF) was a local county and surrounding community organization for kids. Each Monday, about 300 of these youngsters ranging in ages from five to twelve would descend on the lake and proceed to cause lifeguards ulcers. This program was a favorite of Mr. Pfafflin and he immersed himself each Monday into the intricate details of swimming lessons and general upheaval.

I admired the courage and patience of the many young untrained swimming instructors as they struggled to maintain order and accomplish the near impossible. I began to appreciate Father Urban more and more. After the swimming lessons ended, the kids were allowed to play at their leisure until their time was up. These leisure times were the times that tried men's souls. It usually happened in the early part of the season near the front dock. The water in front of the dock was about two feet deep gradually becoming deeper along the sides of the dock reaching a depth of about twelve feet in the back under the diving boards. It was this area along the sides, where the main slide was, that reigned havoc on our nervous systems.

Each Monday morning they would roll in on buses. Into the water they came *reeking of bubble gum and suntan lotion,* totally oblivious to any danger.

As a kid, it seemed reasonable to assume that being able to comfortably touch bottom in the front of the dock, that it would be the same depth everywhere. Unless familiar with the lake from previous experience, it was quite easy for a kid to get in over his/her head, especially by going down the side slide or off the low board.

We were usually fully manned, and one Monday in early June I was assigned to one of the front dock positions in the area between the side slide and the low board. I later named this area the "morgue." It began slowly as the kids meandered ever so diligently from the shallow area up onto the dock, down the slide, and off the board into the unforgiving darkness. The best way to watch this situation was to wait and ensure that what went down came up. Eleven times that day, they did not. The worst case scenario was when two sisters went off the three meter board together, and the only thing that came up was a hair clip. I was lucky and was able to grab both of them just as I hit the water. This went on for about two hours. At the end of the day, the boss congratulated me and patted me on the back. I wanted to smack him.

We all got one weekday off and all tried each year to get Mondays off. No such luck. Mondays were reserved for the NYF, much to the glory and satisfaction of Mr. Pfafflin. The NYF was his baby. No compromises were allowed. But it was all worth it, for at the end of the season, the NYF gave each full-time guard a generous cash bonus, which for most of us in college was sufficient to buy a year's worth of college text books.

I later learned that scary day netted me a pleasant surprise. The following Sunday, Mr Pfafflin told me I had good instincts, and assigned me to the CENTER DOCK with Dan. A dream fulfilled. I had finally made it. I sat there all day twirling my whistle watching the swings, watching the boards, watching the swimmers trying to make it to the dock, with security being provided on week-ends compliments of the 101st Airborne.

Their antics went on all day. By the time I got home that evening, I was so overcome with both joy and exhaustion that I listened to three hours of Bo Diddley music. I thought I could rest on my laurels the rest of the season, but I was in for another surprise, again compliments of the NYF.

The following Monday morning, as I once again prepared mentally for the "morgue," Mr Pfafflin called me aside and asked what I thought of starting a junior lifesaving class for the older NYF youths. I thought it a great idea, since that might reduce our work load on the front dock. I envisioned one of the YMCA/YWCA instructors taking on the burden. I was almost in shock when he told me to prepare for the class, that it would begin the following week, and I was to be the lead instructor.

After work I went to Art & Helen's, a popular college student hangout in Evansville, and consumed 5 beers in rapid succession, and listened to more Bo Diddley music that evening. I felt as if I were about to fall prey to the Peter Principle. All went well however. The course was completed without incident in four weeks, with the final test being given on the fifth week. Under pressure from unheard voices from above, or rather, from Mr Pfafflins' watch stand, all passed with flying colors.

It was an unusually hot summer that year which brought out huge crowds, especially on weekends. It also brought out the bees. Both beaches were loaded with those little white plants that bees love to embrace. They would lie in wait for me and unload at the most inappropriate times. My foot would always swell up to the size of a watermelon. But not all was pain and frustration. Along with every bee sting, came one of the most revered and sacred Pfafflin Lake lifeguard traditions…water foot soothing.

As we struggled with bee sting swelling and pain while sitting on our chairs, little girls ranging in age from nine to twelve would form into work teams of three or four, and would take turns pouring cold water onto the effected foot followed by a light foot massage. They would continue this, sometimes for hours, until the swelling subsided. This act was considered an honor, and carried with it free soft drinks and candy bars for the teams.

I'm sure that today, such activity would warrant CNN scrutiny and a prison sentence. However in those days, those innocent acts constituted part of the mystic of Pfafflin lake.

On slower days when I was assigned the center dock, I began to devise ways to exercise and stay loose. Dan taught me a wonderful exercise involving upper body strength. I would wrap my arms around one of the supporting beams on the dock and throw my body into a perfect horizontal position, and while defying all forces of gravity, hold it there indefinitely. It took most of the summer to perfect this little act of showmanship, and to all beholders a wondrous work of art. I believe he and I were the only ones who could do it with grace and finesse.

The Titanic

DURING SERIOUS RESCUES Mr. Pfafflin would back us up with his motor boat. He was never more than thirty seconds away if needed. One day, I came off the center dock to assist two girls trying to make it across the lake from the north beach to the south beach. They never called out for help but I could usually tell when fatigue slowly reared its ugly head, and the struggle began. I hit the water as Mr. Pfafflin started his boat. We were almost in the center of the lake and here I was with two little girls, one of which was a bit on the hefty side, both grabbing me and trying to climb on top of my head. But fear not, the boat was on the way, or was it? He ran out of gas after about twenty feet.

All was not lost, however, the moment the motor stopped, two other guards hit the water; the crisis was resolved and we all lived to swim another day. I recall that I had accumulated about thirty saves by the end of my second year. I don't think anyone had a real serious situation. We all supported each other and more often than not, each save was accomplished by two guards. However the worst was yet to come the following summer.

The crowds continued to grow throughout the summer as the heat index rose. Bee stings set a record, and Koufax was unbeatable on the mound. I was comfortable in my environment and proud of my swimming skills. Having worked on strength and endurance, I felt I was a somewhat accomplished swimmer by early July, until I entered a river race. In Evansville, the Ohio River runs just south of the city. The principle access to the river for boaters is an area near downtown known as Dress Plaza.

One mile east of this area is a popular beach area known at that time as Sandy Point. The race was held on a Saturday morning and I was given that morning off to participate. The race would begin at Sandy Point and end at Dress Plaza. Each swimmer was accompanied by a boat, compliments of the Evansville Boating club. There were thirty participants. I was confident I could finish in the top ten. I finished twenty-ninth. But wait, it wasn't my fault. Up to that point in my swimming career no one had told me my crawl stroke was right arm dominant. This means I pulled stronger with my right arm than my left. The result being, that if I couldn't see my objective, and swam with my eyes closed, I would swim in a wide circle.

The gun sounded and off we went. I couldn't see the end, so I elected to close my eyes and settle in at a semi-comfortable cruise speed. After about ten minutes, I began to hear my boater yell at me. I thought he was cheering me on. In any event, I was not about to stop. Full of confidence and certain that I was contending well, I kept going, and going, and going, and going. Certainly I had to be getting close. The screams from my boater increased in intensity, so I finally decided to stop and ascertain the nature of his distress. Much to my surprise, Dress Plaza was behind me, and I was nearly on the Kentucky shore line. The unthinkable had happened. Instead of taking the direct route, my right side dominance had taken me on the great circle route, forcing a river barge to stop and an emergency notice to all boaters to be on the lookout for a wayward swimmer.

I very quickly headed in the opposite direction and finished just ahead of the last swimmer. I was told I had finished twenty ninth in the mile race, but had finished first in the two mile race.

That event caused a lot of laughs through the years, much to my chagrin. I immediately planned on working on my dominance problem. I intended to ask the assistance of my college's swim team coach that winter.

By late summer, I had perfected the art of whistle twirling, or so I thought. This is a sacred skill practiced by all lifeguards throughout the world. The objective is to be able to twirl a whistle attached to a rope or other flexible supporting material around the index finger without any other finger touching the rope, wrapping the entire entourage around your finger, and then undoing it in reverse. Many a whistle was lost attempting this feat. My worse disaster occurred on an otherwise calm Thursday afternoon, when much to my surprise while nearly at the end of segment one of the twirl, I lost the whole thing with the whistle flying off and striking a middle school math teacher in the mouth chipping his tooth. After that, I only practiced when I was on the center dock during the week with no swimmers around.

The Vietnam War was becoming more of a problem for the United States. I was in ROTC and therefore not subject to the draft. But more and more non-college types were being drafted. This became a major problem at the lake due to the fact that more soldiers from Fort Campbell, Kentucky, were showing up taking advantage of the loose alcohol environment of beer hill, and thus causing a lot of headaches for Mr. Pfafflin.

This environment attracted ever increasing bad elements. The result being that the north beach was becoming heavily inhabited on weekends. We had to go to extra guards, and by the end of my second year I found myself assigned on weekends to the center guard position on the north beach. I was told they needed my good eyes in that area.

I felt good about it, although the rescues required longer and more riskier swims, I was comfortable and enjoyed my new environment. I was assigned there for the first time on the second to last Sunday of the season. I took a little portable radio, a nice big towel to cover up with, and a small jug of water. Triumphantly, I climbed up, did a couple of whistle twirls and again, promptly got stung by a bee. I couldn't win.

Another problem we had was driving speed. This was quickly resolved with the installation of speed bumps. Many beer hill inhabitants placed their beer in coolers in the trunk of their cars. One day an unsuspecting mob of semi-illiterate fools hit a speed bump at an obscene rate of speed. The resulting spectacle reverberated throughout the entire county. The convertible car flew up, along with the trunk, ejecting three cases of beer along with two back seat occupants over the road with most of the beer flying into the lake, whereupon the driver was quoted as saying, "We must have hit something." A small but significant victory had been achieved.

Those days on the guard chair gave me ample opportunities to continue to reflect on my life and the world. I was in college, most likely headed for a military career, and certain to be affected by the Vietnam War in some way. It seemed to me that the country was losing its conscience. The Cuban missile crisis suggested that we could no longer control events. Events were beginning to control us. The political situation in Washington regarding the Vietnam War began to call attention to the fact that not all was as it should be. People had become agitated.

Young people, convinced that their liberal thinking and pathetic world of drugs, free love, and Volkswagen buses would result in revolution, offered glimpses of things to come. Our sense of humor was vanishing, replaced by anger, fear and uncertainty, as the status quo began to crumble. I felt the times were indeed changing, or was it possible that I was changing. One ponders many things when sitting in a guard chair.

Through those lifeguarding years as I witnessed the slow undoing of our society, I began to appreciate the little things life offered more than ever before: The sunsets at closing time, the smell of the freshly mowed grass, the taste of a Payday candy bar and Pepsi on a hot day and the soothing actions of the bee sting teams. Maybe I could hide from the world. I felt content, at least for the moment. However, these thought patterns would soon be shattered by an event which will live forever in the annals of Pfafflin Lake, as well as my family, the day my mother drove my car into the lake.

I don't recall the circumstances resulting in my mother picking me up at the lake, but near the end of my shift, there she was. The entry to the lake area from the ticket booth was a downhill grade at the end of which was a row of railroad ties separating the parking area from the water's edge. As I recall that day, I was on the center dock contemplating the meaning of life and the role that bikini bra cups played in my on-going attempts to understand the inner workings of the female mind, when out of the gathering mist came my mother and little brother down the hill in my 1952 Dodge.

Her approach to the parking area at first seemed normal, but to my horror, I began to sense a feeling of impending doom; she wasn't slowing down. Through the parking lot she came, and like a German Panzer tank, jumped the railroad ties and hit the water, submerging the car up to the top of the hood. Had it not been for the quick actions of several strong-bodied passersby, and Mr Pfafflin's tractor, my car may have ended up at the bottom of the lake forever. Was this the end of my lifeguarding career? Would I ever live through this? What did my future hold when events such as this permeated my life? Would I be forced to don flowery shirts and become a hippie? That event reignited a sense of humor among all those who witnessed it.

For some reason, I was held in high regard, for my mother had somehow restored our sense of normalcy and clearly demonstrated that life indeed needed to be cherished and not taken so seriously. No explanation was ever forth coming from my mother on what caused her actions that day, and I chose to calmly let the matter pass without further ado. I was convinced it wasn't alcohol related as she was a strict non-drinker. All thought the ordeal was humorous. I did not!

A couple years later, as I was embarking on another car purchase, I overheard her mentioning to my dad words to the effect that whatever I purchased she hoped it would have good brakes. I was satisfied.

That car was not just a car; it was an adventure. It had a few minor discrepancies, like no brakes, no windshield wipers and sadly lacking in lighting, both internally and externally. All three of these functions disappeared one night while I was giving a tour to my girlfriend, her younger sister, and my younger brother through a nearby park in Kentucky.

Audubon Park sits north of Henderson, Kentucky, just off highway 41 and offered a wide array of year round activities. One of its amenities was a scenic perimeter drive. On one of my days off from the lake, the aforementioned group spent that afternoon picnicking and taking in the sites and sounds of this lovely country setting. Before we knew it, darkness was settling in, along with a build-up of storm clouds and related thunder and lightning.

We decided to take the long way out along the dark and curvy perimeter road. The first evidence of pending disaster was revealed in the absence of about 95% of my braking power. Being young and of sound mind, I knew this minor obstacle of mechanical ineptitude could be overcome. As we neared the exit point, confident in my driving skills, the deluge began. It was so bad it rained sideways and further contributed to the braking problem. I thought back to what the pilgrims must have experienced on their transatlantic crossings without the benefit of windshield wipers. I found out ten seconds later when to my ever increasing anxiety, I discovered I had only one functioning windshield wiper. This car was beating me.

By the time we had crossed over the Ohio River into Evansville, it was dark. I reached for the light switch-no lights. My girlfriend was near panic, the kids in the backseat were screaming, and I was driving with my head hanging out the window. About a mile from my girl friend's house with my brakes about 99% ineffective, we began to devise an exit strategy for the girls. My girlfriend's house sat at the bottom of a hill next to a drainage ditch. Whenever it rained hard, the entire end of her street would flood. There was no way I would be able to stop going downhill, and I had to avoid the flood water. An exit strategy was devised posing the least amount of impact on all concerned.

Slowing down to the maximum degree possible, I drove the car up onto her front lawn, and at the right moment the girls jumped out while the car continued to move. I made a sweeping 180 degree turn in her yard, and gunned it out of harm's way. It had worked. Somehow my brother and I made it home, convinced in the existence of guardian angels.

The summer of my first year, my dad had picked the car up for me and had driven it to the lake to pick me up. On the way home, I ran over and killed an Irish Setter. That winter, the car had frozen up resulting in a cracked block, requiring a new motor. By the following summer, shortly after the Audubon Park debacle, I traded the "Titanic," as it was now referred to, in on a beautiful 1956 Ford Crown Victoria. This was the car of my dreams. It burned almost as much oil as it did gas.

I was reminded of this fact when one day the following summer, for some reason, Steve Duncan and I drove separate cars to the lake. He was following me. Just in front of Harrison High School, I sped up in an attempt to moderately intimidate his 1957 Chevy. The resulting trail of oil emanating from my exhausts was so thick that, Steve, ever so humbled, but not to be outdone, turned on his windshield wipers. The following day I began a search for my third car.

Majestic Creature

THE LAKE WAS LAID OUT in such a manner as to attract a host of activities. One could fish away from the noise of the swimming area or enjoy a family picnic throughout the many acres in complete isolation if so desired. There was even an island containing a volleyball court and covered dance pavilion complete with juke box. The boating area was on the eastern part of the lake, and although access to it required passing through the swimming area, it still offered opportunity for peace, quiet, and privacy; opportunities, which I took advantage of during my days off.

That summer Laurie L. was my favorite lake mate. She was an expert in charcoaling chicken wrapped in aluminum foil. She suited my tastes enormously. We had met in high school at a Civil Air Patrol meeting. She looked great in a bikini; we were crazy for each other and loved to frolic at the lake. One July Wednesday on my day off, Laurie and I ventured out into the boating area for a few hours of romantic interlude. We curled up at the bottom of the boat in typical pretzel fashion and proceeded to discuss worldly events. Such things were common occurrence in the boating area, and the inability for anyone to see human activity within a boat was no cause for concern.

All was well. We were having a grand ole time, enjoying the rays, analyzing cloud formations, and discussing the wonders of the world. At a certain point we decided to consume our snacks and wet our whistles with Double Cola. As I reached for the little cooler, I noticed at the opposite end of the boat underneath one of the rubber seats, what appeared to be a bundle of old rags. Closer examination revealed the rags to be a medium sized water moccasin. It raised its head, said hello, I threw a peanut butter and jelly sandwich at it, said goodbye, grabbed Laurie, and over the side we went.

I had two choices, neither of them good. I could pull the boat to the nearest bank, climb up onto fertile soil and hope the invader departed or calmly pull the boat back to the dock and quietly dispose of the problem. I chose neither option. Waving frantically, toward the center dock, I was able to gain the attention of the guard. He yelled at Mr Pfafflin words to the effect that "Wally was in trouble". The motor boat soon arrived and pulled us in.

The snake was disposed of, and again, many enjoyed another round of laughter at my expense. I always suspected that this whole episode was a Cindy Barnes practical joke, for each time she saw me the rest of the summer she would giggle. It seemed that the snake incident fueled Laurie's attraction toward me to even greater heights. Maybe we were bound together forever, but probably not!

Later that summer, Laurie's parents moved to Pompano Beach, Florida. I was invited down over New Year's break and took advantage of the opportunity to get away for a few days. A fun time was had by all. They had an indoor swimming pool. I learned to play canasta, and on New Years' Eve, Laurie, her sister and I went to a nightclub called The House of Pegasus. The band played anti-war protest songs along with a few folk ballads. It seemed that all bands at that time were emulating Peter, Paul and Mary. On the way home we were slightly sideswiped by a hit and run driver, putting a large dent in the driver's side door. We all spent the next two days looking for the culprit of this dastardly deed.

On the night before I left to come home, Laurie suggested we go for a walk around her neighborhood. We ended up underneath a small bridge which spanned a stream. Laurie began telling me how much she wanted to leave home and settle down somewhere. The conversation turned to the subject of marriage. I then knew what the ultimate purpose of this stroll was about. I was in no way ready to get married at that stage in my life.

The next day, I bid farewell and got the hell out of Dodge. Laurie and I communicated with each other for the next few months, but gradually the letters stopped coming, and that was the end of that. Laurie would have made a good marriage partner, but the timing was a bit off. Besides, my mother didn't like her. That night under that bridge got me to thinking about a lot of things. Maybe I should have grabbed the opportunity and run with it.

I thought a lot of Laurie and her family; we had had a lot of fun, but yet I couldn't shake the feeling that I was being manipulated. Maybe I was immature, afraid, or just plain stupid. Perhaps this was another turning point in my life. I would have to work this out in my mind over the next summer while on the guard stand. It would not be my last experience with a bridge.

Steve Duncan could still beat me in the crawl stroke. The more I tried, the faster he got. I had to do something about this. Perhaps I could copy his technique and use it against him. When Steve swam, he would angle his huge hands almost at a ninety degree angle. As he stroked, his hands would enter the water first, followed by his arm. This technique generated tremendous pulling force. Maybe I could do this. I vowed to emulate his technique and use it against him.

Each day for the next week and a half, I practiced the Duncan hand technique angling my hands down as far as I could. After doing this for nine days, I resolved to spend my Wednesday day off in constant hand down swimming. I started at about eleven that morning, swam almost constantly for three hours, took a thirty minute break, then went again for another two hours as hard as I could, all the time angling my hands in Duncan fashion. All the time Steve sat on the center dock with a sheepish grin on his face. I thought to myself that "Someday I'm going to get you boy."

Three o'clock the following morning, my parents were contemplating taking me to the emergency room. My forearms, wrists and hands looked like Popeye's. They had swelled to twice normal. Several aspirins later, the swelling subsided, and I was able to make it to work the next day in time for the noon shift. I got a few strange stares as I reported to work with my wrists wrapped in ice.

If I was ever going to beat him, I would have to do it with brute force. So I slid back into my normal speed and endurance drills, determined that one day I would reign supreme over those giant hands.

It was in late June of that year when I had the daylights scared out of me. It was a relatively quiet Sunday afternoon. I was in my usual position on the north beach when suddenly I sensed movement to my left. Near the eastern end of the beach, on the other side of the bathhouse, the ground slopes downward rather abruptly behind the lake ending in a tree line. The red vehicle gathered speed as it began its uncontrolled journey over the edge of the parking lot, careening off the wall of the bathhouse, and down the slope. All I heard was the sound of tree limbs breaking, followed by a puff of smoke. Surely there had to be serious injuries or fatalities.

I feared that perhaps an entire family had been wiped out. Much to my relief, the car had been unoccupied, had come out of parking gear, and somehow had escaped major damage. That evening, I switched from Bo Diddley to Duane Eddy. It had not been a good year for brakes.

I was accosted that year by my old high school girl friend. Again, it was a Sunday on the north beach, and having just lost another battle with the bees I was standing next to the chair with my foot wrapped in ice. The bee sting relief team was forming when to my sudden surprise the little sister of my ex- girl friend appeared and unloaded a huge biting slap on my butt. I guess this was her way of saying hello. I must have reacted or said something which was in bad taste, and she walked off.

Moments later, I felt the strange sensation I was about to die. It felt as if fire was descending from the heavens and I was about to be recast into a rubber boat filled with snakes. My ex grabbed me by my love handles and for five minutes loosed forth a volley of fire and brimstone. When it was over, I could hear Duncan laughing on the middle dock. I flipped him the bird and climbed back up onto the chair to further ponder the inner workings of the female psyche.

That night I was so overwhelmed by thoughts of women that I could hardly sleep. Why was it so difficult for women to just have fun, enjoy male company without manipulation, evaluation, or judgment? Laurie L. and Karen B. were the closest to meeting my perception of a perfect mate. I began to appreciate how some societies arrange marriages with mates being assigned to you by elders.

Instead of going through all this meeting, going out, and talking underneath bridges crap, on one's eighteenth birthday a mate would be issued to you for life. That would be nice, as long as they liked each other. I didn't think that would work in our country.

By August, I felt sufficiently confident in my swimming that I decided on a feat never accomplished at the lake up to that time. With permission granted from the boss, on a slow day, I took off on a swim around the entire perimeter of the lake. It was one of the most enjoyable swims I have ever had. Even to this day, I look back on that feat not as some high achievement, which it wasn't, but rather as a gift to myself celebrating the joys of lake life. I used a slow crawl stroke and enjoyed immensely the sublime feeling of freedom. I was at home in the water and totally content. I felt as though all the struggles and frustrations of my life up to that point had been worth it, just to experience those few minutes of peaceful utopia.

My crawl stroke had improved immensely, but I was still too slow, and probably a little too heavy to keep up with the leaner guys. I continued to work on endurance by surface diving to the bottom, resurface, swim about ten yards, then repeat, across the lake and back. I knew I was getting stronger, but not faster.

And so another year ended. A lot had occurred. Life at the lake had not taken on any new dimensions. I had decided to take advantage of the pool in the new Carson Center Sports Center on my college campus. I had to overcome my swimming deficiencies. It was during those winter months that I began to notice my worsening eyesight and a dull pain in my right side.

I played football in high school. In my junior year, just two days prior to our first game, I had awakened early in the morning with an intense pain in my right side. I had a fever of 104, and according to my mom, was pale as a ghost. A call to the family doctor resulted in an immediate trip to the Saint Mary's Hospital emergency room.

I was x-rayed, probed, examined, x-rayed again and had my blood drawn at least four times. Nothing was found. I remained hospitalized for five days. My doctor suspected a possible ruptured spleen, with internal bleeding although nothing showed up in that regard.   In any case, after some medication, I was discharged and advised to sit out the rest of the season and see what developed.

I played football again in my senior year, but it seemed my athletic skills had diminished and I spent most of that season on the bench. Something was wrong.

Canine Caper

AS THE NEW EVANSVILLE COLLEGE SWIM TEAM began its workouts; I asked Coach Nick Voorhees if I could participate in the early season practice and conditioning sessions in an attempt to overcome my right side dominance problem. It worked. Although not nearly possessing the speed and endurance of the regular team members, I did manage to keep up with most of the drills, and in so doing, became a much stronger and straighter swimmer.

Coach Voorhees pointed out another weakness of which I was unaware. He noticed that the power of my crawl stroke kick was greatly diminished due to the structure of my legs. It seemed that my left foot would angle out ninety degrees from my right foot, thus contributing to less thrust. I worked on that, as well as my breathing techniques. My major weaknesses were corrected. However, another problem began to emerge. I began to gain weight.

When the competition portion of the college swimming season began, I thanked coach Voorhees and spent the remaining off season working out with weights and playing intramural sports for my fraternity.

Center Dock

On campus swimming was one of those sports. I had always had a good breast stroke due to my body build. I was just sway backed enough, that the breast stroke came easy for me. I had made the finals for that year's intramural breast stroke event. Ironically, my main competition was Bob Dodge, who having recovered from his accident, was back in swimming form. I had heard he was a tremendous swimmer and was somewhat of an icon at the lake during his lifeguarding days.

I thought I could beat him. At the sound of the gun, we took off reaching the far wall evenly matched; with a perfectly executed turn and wall kick, I surged ahead. As the other contenders fell back, I glanced to my right; we were in a dead heat. I gave it all I had down the stretch; he pulled ahead just a bit for a second then faltered- we were again neck and neck. He touched one tenth of a second before I did.

That fall the intramural red-flag football season began. Being both a member of the college ROTC program and my fraternity, I was torn by indecision on the day the ROTC was playing my fraternity. Not using my head and laying this one out, I opted to play for my fraternity. I played defensive nose guard.

All through the game I kept stupidly taunting their offense, daring them to run over the middle. This went on for most of the game. With about thirty seconds remaining we were down by a touchdown. They had the ball on the four yard line, fourth down. If we could stop them, we still had a chance to tie the game. We lined up close and tight; the ball was snapped and eleven screaming maniacs came at me with the power of an uncontrolled bulldozer.

The laughter from the sidelines brought me to my senses, and as I lay there on my back in the mud, I was reminded of a poster that hung in my high school football coach's office. This poster depicts a football player exiting the field and being talked to by his coach. The player is beaten to a pulp with his face all bloody, uniform torn and hanging in shreds, and outlines of footprints extending from head to toe. The caption underneath reads, "Where were you on that play Ferguson?"

I exited the field suffering another example of humility and forever embracing the elegance of keeping one's mouth shut.

The third summer had everything. I met and dated several lovely ladies, most of whom I knew from college. I was happy with my swimming skills. College, although a struggle for me academically, was nevertheless progressing. Even the dreaded Mondays at the lake seemed to be getting easier. I was on top of the world, and king of the north beach.

I felt as though I had been knighted by the Queen herself when on that early July morning, Mr. Pfafflin informed me I was to help set off fireworks from the center dock that Fourth of July. I had come full circle from a skinny seven-year-old jumping off the kiddy dock to center dock lighter of fireworks. All else was insignificant. When the big night arrived, Danny and I began by setting a few boomers off from atop the twenty-seven foot platform. Each sequence culminated in a feet first leap into the black depths. I couldn't even see the water that night. The twenty-seven footer was no longer a challenge, as it became routine to do the paratrooper bit at least once a day. I was truly in my element. For the next hour, we proceeded to light up the sky and create fond memories that would last a lifetime.

It was that summer that a few problems began to erode the morale among the crew. The primary cause was volleyball. Danny and the other two Steves were avid volleyball players. The volleyball court on the island was often the scene of extended duals in the sand. Our shifts and manning were arranged in such a manner that every two hours, each guard would get a fifteen-minute break. The intent was to allow the guys to cool off in the shade, get hydrated, and if desired take a swim to stay loose.

These breaks eventually evolved into thirty- to forty- minute volleyball games. This was no problem on rainy days or slow week days, but on hot weekends, these breaks took on serious implications. Sunstroke was an ever-present danger, along with sun headaches and dehydration. We didn't have umbrellas on our stands, so we were left to our own protection devices, which in most cases consisted of a large towel. Breaks were essential. On numerous occasions, the expected breaks did not occur on schedule due to the volleyball activity. Mr Pfafflin finally had to intervene to keep us from tearing out each other's throats.

I blame Milton Purdie for a lot of the volleyball goings-on at the lake. I believe volleyball played a major role in his life. He would organize most of the volleyball challenges and would spend each weekend and some weekdays at the lake playing volleyball the entire day. He was a tremendous athlete.

I knew Milton's wife Eileen. She and I worked together at Wesselman's Supermarket in Evansville when I was in high school.

One day, I was at the lake on my day off. Milt was there, but no volleyball players were available, so he challenged me to a quick game of one-on-one. Already aware of my complete ineptitude toward the game, he offered to play with one hand behind his back, and allowed me both hands and one bounce. How could I possibly lose? I lost 21-7. He was that good.

I occasionally played volleyball on my breaks and learned a few fundamentals of serving and setting the ball. One of my little skills I developed was serving the ball high and dropping it just over the net. To the opponent, the ball looked as if it would fall short, but would just barely miss the top of the net and drop in. Little did I know that those days would manifest themselves in unbelievable fashion fourteen years later.

In 1977, I was assigned for the second time to Fort Lee, Virginia. One day, I noticed a memo on the bulletin board asking for volleyball players to play on the local Air Force team. Apparently, another version of Milt Purdie was assigned and was putting together a volleyball team for intramural competition with the Army teams. I tried out. I didn't start every game, but my setting skills and serving technique learned at the lake years before proved invaluable, as our team went undefeated for five years.

I continued playing volleyball in the military, and was on another local championship team while stationed in Taiwan.

The beer hill situation continued to deteriorate. Drunken brawls were common occurrences on the weekends. The Fort Campbell crowd scared off the majority of the law abiding clientele, and the north beach was slowly becoming what resembled a police state. The county sheriff was often called to help quell the unrest and haul away the trouble makers. Mr. Pfafflin eventually called the provost marshal at Fort Campbell and demanded assistance in controlling the Fort Campbell situation. The result was that each weekend that summer and several summers afterward saw the presence of military MP's and county sheriff deputies.

It all began to take a toll on the Pfafflin family. I began to notice an increase in the irritability of Mr. Pfafflin. In the years I worked at that lake, Mr. Pfafflin seemed to have aged twenty years. His presence at the lake began to decrease, and he appeared more and more exhausted. I knew that summer that the era of Pfafflin Lake was coming to an end. I estimated three more years. I was wrong!

Besides his lake, Mr. Pfafflin had another love-hunting dogs. He had several award winning beagles. His favorite was a champion beagle ironically named Champion. That dog was his prized possession. He had about twenty dogs, all bred for rabbit hunting. Near the end of the swimming day he would come down the hill with five or six dogs all hot on the trail of some critter. Those dogs were granted the run of the lake, and inevitably after about ten minutes, we would hear that unmistakable howl of a beagle on the trail of a rabbit. Mr. Pfafflin could stand on the south beach, with the dogs in the woods behind the north beach and could tell which dog had the scent merely by his bark. That had to take dedication.

One rainy day, we were tasked with clearing dead trees and brush. I was getting the tractor from behind the Pfafflin residence and decided to have a close look at the dog kennels. My presence created quite a stir as all dogs showed their affection in the most intense manner. Two of the dogs were also in the act of showing affection toward each other. They appeared to be glued together at the rump facing away from each other. A closer look revealed that they at that moment were either attempting or finishing up the act of doggy copulation, and had somewhat become twisted around and were unable to disengage. They looked like the proverbial two-headed llama. They continued that way for some time, and I didn't know if this was normal activity, or if this was God's way of telling me that perhaps my sex education had left something out. In an attempt to hide my ignorance on this matter, I chose to not tell anyone. I wonder what ever happened to those dogs.

Mr. Pfafflin loved the water and had a unique skill that to this day I have never been able to duplicate. The man would enter the water, swim out to the center of the lake then slowly rotate over onto his back and float perfectly motionless and sleep for a couple hours. He reminded me of an alligator. Many times, the guards would be alerted about the man floating in the water.

It was near closing time one weekday afternoon, and I was on the center dock. This middle-aged lady had swum out to the center dock and after climbing up the ladder asked very quietly if she could speak with me. I asked what I could do for her. She very softly and sincerely whispered in my ear that there was a dead body floating over yonder in the water. I decided to have a little fun, and whispered back to her that we usually had several dead bodies that surface about this time each day and that we merely collected them at closing time and put them in the bath house, until the coroner came for them.

At the end of the shift, Mr. Pfafflin asked me what I had said to that lady. It seems that she was a retired FBI agent, and had related my tale to him, and that she was concerned. We all had a good laugh.

I never saw that lady at the lake again.

Mrs. Pfafflin was a joy to be around. It was obvious that she was the power behind the power. She was the minister of finance for the lake operations and handled our pay and concession accounts and I'm sure a host of other family financial matters. We got along splendidly. On slow days we enjoyed many a quick homemade snack in the concession stand. I will never forget her warm down-home smile. However, it was that year that I also began to notice a slight change in Mrs. Pfafflin. She slowed down considerably and began to exhibit signs of fatigue. How much longer could these people do this?

It was about this time in my life guarding career that I began to experience the joy of solitude. The weekdays were in no way as crowded as the weekends and offered opportunities to ponder my surroundings on slow days. Some of my fondest recollections were the quiet moments spent on the center dock waiting for the occasional swimmer. I could hear the water lapping against the dock and spot an occasional fish pass by. On stormy days I could feel the breezes cooling your face and watch the clouds forming up in the west followed by the beginnings of unimaginable sunsets. Those were the moments I will always cherish the most. I somehow gained strength from this solitude immersed in nature at its purest form. I wanted to sit there forever.

Limestone Loonies

IF BOB DODGE AND SIGMA ALPHA EPSILON fraternity thought that the one tenth of one second victory was to go unanswered they were sadly underestimating my competitive mentality. One night the following spring semester a few of us guitar-minded guys had gathered in the men's dorm to discuss the idea of putting together a band. Not all of us were in fraternities, and one particular individual, although a good friend from our high school football days, was somewhat anti-fraternity. The conversation turned to the fraternity rivalries we were experiencing on campus at that time. My fraternity, Tau Kappa Epsilon, had a friendly rivalry with the SAE's primarily due to the intramural sports competition; however, our rivalry with Sigma Phi Epsilon bordered on downright hatred. This group had pulled numerous dirty tricks on us over the years.

I don't recall the exact conversation, but I do remember the result-we were going to get even with both fraternities. It was to be accomplished with paint and a pregnant skunk.

In the front yard of the SAE house was a large statue of a lion. The lion was significant in SAE history. It resembled marble, but I wasn't sure of its makeup. I don't recall its color, but it didn't matter, it was about to become a lion of a different color. We waited until about one in the morning. I drove the getaway car. Pulling into the Shell station area next door, my anti-fraternity friend proceeded to cover the lion in a bright hot pink luster.

We took off in a cool but deliberate manner and proceeded along our planned escape route. I couldn't believe we were actually doing this. We pulled into the designated safe spot and waited to see if anyone was in pursuit. After about thirty minutes, we called a halt to our shenanigans and proceeded to our safe havens. One down, and one to go.

The next day, all talk on campus centered around the new décor in the SAE yard. Who could possibly have done such a thing. Still worried that somehow we would be ratted out, I quietly went about my academic business, content in the notion that perhaps we had gotten by with it. We did get by with it.

Thirty nine years later, my wife, daughter and I, after having attended an incoming freshmen and parents' orientation for my college bound daughter, stopped in that same Shell station to gas up. There, next door, in the front yard set the SAE lion in all its dramatic glory. My thoughts returned to that early morning hour so many years ago. No one had ever learned the identity of the hot pink marauders. A feeling of guilt over took me. I decided to be a man, make amends for my actions, and fess-up to my crime. As my wife looked on in understanding concern, and my daughter mentally making preparations for my funeral, I walked up to the front door of the SAE house and knocked.

It was easier than I had anticipated. A young man answered the door; I introduced myself and related to him that I had painted his lion hot pink thirty-nine years earlier, wanted to unload my burden of guilt, and ask for SAE forgiveness. He smiled, shook my hand, told me I was forgiven, and to go forth and sin no more. He then burst my bubble by telling me it hadn't been the only time the lion had experienced a color bath.

After humbling the SAE fraternity, my small army of two laid low for about a month, still waiting for the axe to fall, and planning our next hit. My friend had an uncle who lived out in the county amid numerous critters, including an abundance of skunks. After discussing several scenarios involving paint, stink bombs, rubber snakes, and toilet paper we settled on the idea of giving a home to a wayward skunk. Again, I drove the getaway car. It was just pure luck that one of the windows on the isolated western side of the SIGEP house was open. In went the skunk, and off we went on the same escape route as before. Nothing happened. Another victory; I had been avenged. The midnight marauders had struck again. To those aware of our caper it was a classic and humorous act of vengeance. To the college administration it was something entirely different.

Three weeks later I got called into the Dean of Student's office. As I walked into the limestone administration building, I began to calculate the odds of ever graduating, where I was going to live after my parents threw me out, and what kind a job was in my future. I was told that I had been identified as one of the skunk culprits. Someone had seen my car and ratted us out. We had a choice. Either pay for the damage caused to the SIGEP house or face disciplinary action and possible suspension or even expulsion. We paid the bill of several hundred dollars each. I felt relieved that I had survived and could possibly fight another day.

It seemed that the skunk had enjoyed an unnoticed run of the house for about three days, where upon strange odors began to be noticed. It continued to get worse and about a week later the cause had been identified. It seemed that the skunk had been pregnant and had left her contribution to the skunk world behind the SIGEP chapter room curtain. This area also served as living room, bathroom, kitchen and birthing clinic for Mrs. skunk. In an attempt to fend off starvation, she had used the felt material on the back of the curtain for her nourishment. Her death and the death of her offspring signaled the end of further moonlight excursions by my crew.

The skunk scenario soured me on future pranks. I had done my share. My parents were livid. My fraternity was in defensive mode, and my grades were less than ordinary. I was ready to abandon my childish pursuits, grow up, settle down and vigorously delve into academia. I was soon to be denied that opportunity.

I suppose sibling rivalry is a healthy thing. After reveling in my downfall, and being told by my parents to get serious or get out, my little brother, Tom, challenged me to a feat of unmitigated insanity. We had thought about this stunt for several years, but apparently this was the right time for him to raise me back to a level of respectability, or forever banish me into the abyss. I wasn't sure of his motivation. Perhaps this was his chance for avenging all the times I shoved him out the house while naked and locked the door, or for the time I hung him out our bedroom window by his feet in his underwear in full view of our next door neighbor. In any case, I decided that maybe I had room for one more lunatic act.

Twin bridges over the Ohio River connect Evansville, Indiana and Henderson, Kentucky. One span runs north the other south. There is about a thirty yard-gap between the two structures. Our objective was, when traffic flow was lightest, with one of us on one span and the other on the other span, to toss a football through the beams from one to the other and back again successfully; a nearly impossible feat. Success could only be achieved by both parties catching the ball.

Numerous trips were made over the bridges, mental calculations taken, and the final plan formulated. We were ready. The moment of infamy was at hand. The weather was not ideal; foggy, damp and chilly, yet clear enough for the attempt. We had to move fast. We were in luck-no immediate traffic. We each approached our respective positions, stopped our cars, and exited onto the spans. I would go first. With visions of parental backlash, jail sentences, fines, or even death itself, I took aim and gave the ball a mighty heave. The arc was perfect, the spiral strong and true. The ball sailed upward and through the set of supporting beams of the first span over the gap, and downward toward the second span. If it hadn't been for that final cross beam just inches from the outstretched hands of my brother, a historical accomplishment would have been recorded. The ball careened off the cross beam and disappeared into the blackness below. So close, yet so far.

As I stood there absorbed by the thickening fog, I began to ponder the meaning of this moment. Just what the hell was I doing standing on a bridge, in the fog, in the middle of the night. I had come full circle from a small child throwing pots and pans down the basement stairs, and locking myself in the bathroom, filling the bathtub with water, talcum powder, and toilet paper to this spot on a bridge span. What was it about bridges? It seemed my most intense moments occurred on or under bridges. Why and how do I allow myself to be victimized by these hapless adventures? Was I not allowed to grow up and begin a life of disciplined normalcy? Was this the end of my idiocy? Was this hopeless feat another turning point in my life? Only time would tell.

Later that fall, I once again experienced pain in my right side. It became so intense I couldn't stand up. Another call to the doctor netted another trip to the emergency room. It was easy this time; I had appendicitis. That afternoon, they removed my ruptured appendix and in so doing noticed evidence of past internal bleeding. They did a little exploration and were unable to detect the source. My doctor suspected a torn stomach lining. In any case, I recovered, but had to take heavy doses of weird medicine for two weeks. The strange pain disappeared never to return. To this day, I still don't know the exact cause.

Swimmer Down

I BELIEVE UP TO THAT TIME the lake had experienced only one drowning. I had always feared that due to the nature of the layout of this lake, someday, disaster would strike. We had a large boating area and an even larger swimming area. I constantly worried about the boating area. Lifeguards were not responsible for overseeing the boating area, and it was a struggle to keep boaters from getting into the water too far from their boats and not being able to get back. An attempted rescue would surely result in failure, as the distance to the boating area was at least two hundred yards, and the water depth was about thirty feet.

The only salvation for the boaters was Mr. Pfafflin's motor boat. With all the problems with alcohol and trouble makers, I feared something was about to happen. It did. It didn't occur out in the boating area; it occurred sixteen feet from shore on the far eastern portion of the north beach. He dove into the water, came up once, went down again and disappeared.

That Sunday started off normally. For some reason, the mood was somber going into the early afternoon. No major trouble was reported. All was quiet at Pfafflin Lake. As the crowds began to accumulate, one individual caught the attention of Mr. Pfafflin. He was obviously

Center Dock

not acting normal, and was being watched through binoculars by Mr. Pfafflin from his perch next to the south beach concession stand.

I was on break on the south beach when I heard Mr. Pfafflin yell over his loud speaker system, "Get him Brenner." Charlie Brenner was on the nearest stand, and hit the water followed by two other guards. Danny was on the center dock and yelled, "Swimmer down". Mr. Pfafflin picked up Danny from the center dock in the boat, and I ran around the back side of the lake. By the time I arrived, all north beach guards and several volunteers were diving frantically to no avail. The swimmer had simply vanished.

As I entered the water, I could hear Mildred yelling at me over the intercom from the south beach concession stand. "Wally, come this way ten yards, and to your left another ten yards", down I went- nothing. There was a volunteer next to me, and I suggested we go another ten yards further out; down we went-nothing. When we came up, the volunteer told me he thought he had touched a foot. Someone yelled, "Over here," someone else yelled, "Ok we need four guys; let's go." We found him just below me in about ten feet of water. He was blue with no response. Danny worked on him for about fifteen minutes. I relieved Danny and continued for another fifteen minutes. It was the first time I used CPR in an actual emergency. He was gone. Mr. Pfafflin called a halt to our efforts.

The victim's name was Herbert Dale Pruitt.

I was surprised at how quickly we all recovered from the drowning tragedy. It was the final week of the season. The NYF business had ended two weeks prior, and we began to wind down the operation. Boats were deflated and stored in the boat storage building. Picnic tables were collected and prepared for painting, and the guard chairs were placed inside the bath houses. It was during one of these picnic table inspection trips that I experienced another snake incident.

Near the end of the season, some of us were sent to the north side picnic area to inspect picnic tables to determine if any needed painting. I approached a table and nearly stepped on a large snake. I didn't have anything with me, so I jumped up onto the table, and yelled across the lake for someone to brink a rake or shovel. Danny drove over with a shovel, and much to my surprise discovered that the source of my panic was dead on arrival. It had not been a good year for snakes. I felt like a wimp and was determined to get my revenge on one of these critters.

I'm not really terrified of snakes unless they end up in my bed. When I was stationed in Italy in the mid 1980s, I was told by my supervisor there were no snakes in the area where I lived. I was also told there were no drunks in Italy, until I saw one get run over by a bus.

I lived in an Italian villa on top of a small hill just east of Lake Garda close to Verona. One day, while mowing grass I saw two small snakes entertaining each other underneath a hedge row in the side yard. Upon relating this citing to my Italian supervisor, I was told I was hallucinating, that there were no snakes in this area. I told him that the Titanic didn't really sink, and that the drunk run over by a bus was really a guy made out of rubber. No wonder they killed Mussolini.

Prior to being stationed in Italy, I was stationed in Oklahoma City where I served as a battle commander on the E3-A AWACS plane. We lived just off base in a real nice sub-division along with a million snakes. One day my three-year-old daughter came running up to me yelling, "Nake, daddy, nake." I immediately knew what she was saying. Just outside the side garage door was the biggest snake I'd ever seen. I thought it was a rattler.

I called my neighbor from down the street to bring his shotgun. He came running loaded for bear and cautiously approached the critter. Upon closer review, he said, "Steve, you big pussy, that's just a harmless bull snake." He picked it up, wrapped it around his arm and released it into the woods across the street. We had contemplated putting it in my next door neighbor's mail box, but decided that good neighborly relations over road serious practical jokes.

After retiring from the military, we lived near Hawesville, Kentucky, on a hill overlooking the Ohio River. Naturally we had as many snakes as we had mice. Our cat controlled the mice population, and my golden retriever would let us know if a snake was nearby. I never bothered any of the Kentucky snakes until one summer night, my wife and I pulled into the garage only to spot a snake trying to enter the house through the inside garage door. I chose to neutralize that critter against the better wishes of my wife. I felt that once a snake sampled human environments that it would seek a permanent home in my bedroom, drink my wine, and eat my fig bars when we were gone.

On the last day, we collected our bonuses, discussed our availability for next year, and bid farewell until next May. I was in a relatively sedate mood until that night when Mr. Pfafflin nearly killed me.

It seemed the drowning left an impression on my newest girl friend. I don't recall her name, but that evening, I decided to accomplish two things. I would sneak in the back road around the west end of the lake out of sight of the Pfafflin residence (or so I thought), and give her a quick tour of the north beach, and maybe engage in a little kissy face-huggy bear activity. I heard the first shot gun blast the moment I pulled into the parking area. How could he know? How could he have seen me? The second blast came just as I was exiting the back access road.

I'm convinced he didn't know who it was, because I had my lights off. I didn't have a girl friend the next day, but from that night on I restricted my evening activities to more healthy pursuits. I couldn't decide which was worse… bees, women, or shotguns. I never heard any mention of the incident, so I assumed I had gotten out unrecognized.

The Water Stalker

MY FINAL YEAR AT THE LAKE was the most memorable. I was well on the road toward graduation. My grades had improved remarkably, and I began to experience a sense of maturity. A lot had happened through my college years. I felt grateful for my position in life, and tended to enjoy things more as I grew out of my shell. The thought of more serious pursuits occupied my mind as I contemplated leaving home and this playground for more worldly pursuits. I knew I had a military obligation after graduation, but beyond that, the jury was still out. I knew one thing for sure. My experiences at the lake would remain with me forever. I felt that it was my destiny to someday return to this place and relive these years over again.

I don't remember the exact makeup of our lifeguarding crew that year. Most of the veterans were back, but I do recall a couple of rookies coming on board. Nothing much else had changed. The operation started off as usual, and the lake enjoyed a quiet season until the middle of July, when it seemed that all the trouble makers appeared at once. Trash barrels were kicked over, quiet folks migrated from the north beach to the south beach, and the alcohol problem took off again.

Center Dock

We all grew weary of it all and began to show signs of burnout. It seemed that most of the veterans were finding solitude in an ever parade of girlfriends. Women were all we talked about. They were everywhere, and for those gifted with the skill, found easy pickings, except me. My current girlfriend at that time was what I refer to as an evaluator. An evaluator is a girl who constantly monitors your every move, your every word, your every breath taken, in an attempt to use it against you, rate you as husband potential or reasons known only to them. It was so sad. She was an absolute knock out, intelligent, and classy. I considered myself fortunate to be attached to her, but in the back of my mind knew I would never meet her standards. It was extremely difficult to please her. I began to grow weary of her rating system and slowly began a permanent retreat.

The girls came and the girls went. Karen B. was my all time favorite girlfriend. We had dated off and on during my senior year in high school and on into my college years. But after I mentioned the possibility of marriage in a few years, she began a disappearing act. Isn't that supposed to be the other way around? I was back to bees and shotgun blasts.

Little did I know what was about to occur.

As the other guys chased the girls, I continued to find peace during my weekday center dock meditations. I experienced my third bee sting that year, and my first case of what we referred to as chair sickness. It was really sun stroke. It was on a hot Sunday afternoon. I had my usual Sunday position on the north beach. It began as a slight ringing in my ears, followed by a feeling of total helplessness. I woke up on the ground surrounded by a throng of people. Mr. Pfafflin was pouring water over me and they had my head encased on a bed of ice. Good lord! I quickly recovered and like being thrown from a horse, climbed back up on the stand and assumed the position. I was not going to be beaten by nature. That evening I had the worst headache of my life.

That Fourth of July witnessed an incident which carried over long after the lake had closed. Mr. Pfafflin had repeatedly warned about setting off firecrackers in the beach area. The problem continued through most of the holiday weekend. The warnings went unheeded. I had had enough. I ost my cool while on a break on the south beach. There was a group of youths ignoring the loudspeaker pleadings of the boss. One of these characters set off a cherry bomb just a few yards from a small child. I threw down my drink, and must have had a most dreadful look on my face, for all I heard the next few moments was, "Oh shit". I was furious.

I walked quickly and in a most deliberate, ungentlemanly manner approached the group, and grabbed the nearest one, and proceeded to manually toss this character from the confines of the beach area, and ordered him off the premises. Thankfully he agreed to depart, but said in no uncertain terms that this was not over. At least the firecracker lighting had stopped. Two years later, I experienced déjà-vu, while having a beer with some of my fraternity brothers at Art and Helen's.

Art and Helens was a combined tavern and café in Evansville on Division Street just off Highway 4. On Friday and Saturday nights our fraternity band played live music in the back room. It met its demise a few years later with the construction of the Lloyd Expressway. I had recently graduated from college, and was preparing to enter the Air Force. A few of us were sitting in one of the café booths when up staggers none other than the fire cracker boy I had tossed out of the lake a few years earlier. He asked if I had ever been a lifeguard at Pfafflin Lake? I responded in the affirmative, whereupon he asked if I had ever thrown anyone out of the lake? I again responded in the affirmative. He told me he was the one I tossed on the Fourth of July one year and that he was not the one who had set off that cherry bomb. He then told me he was drunk and couldn't do anything about it then, but that someday, somewhere in a dark alley that fate would catch up to me.

Over the years, I came to regret my actions that July day. I had lost my temper. I was totally wrong. So, my friend, if you are reading this, I apologize, and hope to make it up to you someday-but not in any alleys. How about over a couple of beers and some barbeque ribs, my treat.

The fireworks activity went off again without a hitch and Danny and I again enjoyed setting off the center dock rockets. However, an ugly and near tragic incident occurred the following weekend involving Mrs. Gardner. After being told to leave the premises, a carload of drunken troublemakers on their way out vented their anger by driving into the ticket booth, destroying the booth and scaring Mrs. Gardner half to death. I knew at that point that the end was near. I could sense it and see it in everyone's eyes.

A year earlier some folks named Kramer had approached the Pfafflins seeking their advice on a lake they were opening for recreational activity near Evansville. Earlier that current summer I had gone to that lake on one of my days off. It's operation and layout was similar to our lake although on a much smaller scale. In the middle of the lake set a center dock similar to ours. They had separate swimming and boating areas, but only one small beach area. It was nice and clean, and I had a good time that day chatting with the guards.

We learned a few days after that Fourth of July, that Kramer Lake had a drowning on the Fourth. Two weeks later Hartke Pool had a drowning. Drownings are like car accidents; they drive up liability insurance rates. I knew it was all taking a toll on Mr. Pffafflin.

She would only swim out to the center dock when there were no other swimmers around, and hang on to the ladder and stare at me. This went on for most of that summer. Why me? I in no way possessed attributes that appealed to women, only bees. She kept getting more brazen as the season went on. She would hang onto the ladder and go through a set of gyrations which reminded me of those damned beagle dogs. I estimated her to be about sixteen and weighing about 160 pounds. She wasn't as much unattractive as she was a nuisance. I began to refer to her as the water stalker. I tried to ignore her actions, as she was way too young for my tastes, and besides I had a negative attitude regarding women during that period in my life. But then she began to talk to me from the confines of the dock ladder. It was beginning to annoy me.

One day she asked me if I had ever wrapped my penis in plastic? Jesus, what was with this girl? The activity began to decrease in episodes but did not end completely. I thought it all was just teenage fantasy until that fall. After that season ended, and with college once again occupying my time, thoughts of the lake had left my mind, until I spotted the water stalker sitting in a car parked just down the street from my house in Evansville.

This went on for nearly a month. Each Friday and Saturday afternoon, there she would sit until after dark. I didn't know whether to feel sorry for her or just ignore her hoping she would go away. Finally, in late September, she vanished. I thought her little act had run its course. I was wrong again!

During my college years I alternated between living in the fraternity house and living at home. Most weekends, primarily due to my love life being on the skids, I stayed at home or went to the Aces basketball games. Whatever the reason, one early evening in October, my parents were at a clabber card party with friends, and my little brother was attending a play at his school. I was getting ready to go to my fraternity's annual fall yard party.

I had just gotten out of the shower, and in all my naked glory opened the bathroom door, and there stood the WATER STALKER!! Oh my god! The defining moment of this caper had finally arrived. Not sure of her intentions, my mind was racing, along with my blood pressure. I envisioned the following morning headlines-LIFEGUARD FOUND DEAD WITH HIS PENIS WRAPPED IN PLASTIC (or even worse). I was determined to get through this with as much dignity as I could muster. I calmly stated that it was nice to see her again, and asked her directly if she wanted to make out a little. She responded with a head nod-sideways, smiled, and calmly walked out my back door and into Pfafflin Lake lore. I breathed a sigh of relief, more conscious of my physical attributes, or lack thereof, than ever before, and convinced that my sex life would forever suffer the pain of mediocrity. I just couldn't win.

That summer, I was determined to beat Steve Duncan in the crawl stroke across the lake. The event took place on a slow Thursday afternoon during a pre-planned break period. How could I be bested after years of hard work, college swim team training, and river race experience against someone who had done nothing in this regard. I was ready!

Mr. Pfafflin enjoyed these spectacles of competition, after all, any swimming activity by his guards was heartily encouraged. We stood on the north shore, and readied for an all out dash across the lake to the opposite shore. Mr. Pfafflin gave the signal, and off we went. The first 20 yards we were equal; I pulled ahead a bit and felt strong, breathing good, path straight, strokes smooth and deliberate. The first thing I realized was how strong I felt. I felt no fatique whatsoever as I reached, pulled and kicked . Suddenly, Duncan's huge hands began to dig in and push back water like a giant thrashing machine. He pulled ahead, and remained there beating me by five yards. What would it take to beat this guy? Mr. Pfafflin thought the whole episode humorous and commented that my failure must be the result of bee venom. He commented that he was impressed with my resolve and obvious improvement of my swimming skills. I had done my best. I was just too fat!

Near the end of that season, a near double drowning occurred. I don't recall their names but the middle-aged couple had been coming to the lake for many years and had been long time Newburgh residents.

It was late afternoon on what had been a crowded Saturday. I was in the chair on the north beach with just a few swimmers. Tom Farrell was on the center dock as a relief guard. I don't know why I was watching the couple since I was on the opposite side of the lake. They were near the rear ladder of the kiddie dock and had begun a slow exodus into the deeper water, headed for the center dock. I was fixated on them. Suddenly they stopped moving, and the lady grabbed her husband. It didn't look right. They were just beyond the reach of the front dock ladder when I stood up in my chair and began motioning to Tom. He was engaged in conversation with a girl and totally oblivious to anything else. I knew we were in trouble when the lady went down and the husband began flailing. I gave a loud hit on my whistle; Tom looked at me as I pointed across the lake. I blew again, pointed and yelled, "God dam it Tom wake up". He turned, spotted the crisis, and hit the water.

Both potential victims were below water by the time he arrived, and with the help of another swimmer, got the couple back to the ladder. That was the first time in my life that I had entertained thoughts of committing murder. I never forgave Tom for that day, and our relationship deteriorated after that to a point of barely acknowledging each other.

Family Genes

AS IF THE EVENTS THAT SUMMER were not enough to alter my mental stability, on a late June night, one of my cousins decided to further damper my sanity by nearly scaring the hell out of me.

To best appreciate the story, it is necessary to understand that I come from a family of dry-witted practical-jokers. We believe it originated in the gene pool of my grandfather. The things my dad pulled on my mom could be made into a television mini-series. My cousin Sharlot inherited this gene to the maximum and used it against me in a fanatical act of horror.

With both her parents having passed on, Sharlot was engaged to be married in a few weeks. She was a favorite niece of my Dad's, and he invited her to live in my parents' new home until her wedding. I was still living at home most of the time, so we all had a great time playing silly games and all the things that families do.

One night, I came home from the lake having worked the late shift. That afternoon was slow so a few of us were tasked with cutting down dead trees, clearing brush and cutting fire wood. I was exhausted when I got home and decided to hit the sack early.

Sharlot, her fiancé and my little brother were in the living room, and all seemed unusually upbeat. I should have recognized the symptoms of another family caper, but I was too tired to engage in any in depth thought processes, I went into my room, switched on the light…no light. I thought the bulb must have been burned out. I got undressed down to my undies and felt around for the bed and thereupon proceeded to pull back the covers and enter the world of peaceful slumber.

I first sensed something was out of the ordinary when I rolled over on my side and felt a leg that wasn't mine. Had I gotten in the wrong bed? Was this a dream? I then felt what I thought was hair. SOMEONE WAS IN MY BED! Oh God, was it the water stalker? I jumped up, felt around and finally found my flashlight in my top dresser drawer and shined a light onto this intruder. There before me lay the most hideous, ugliest creature I had ever seen. It had long stringy hair, only half a nose and one eyeball was hanging out. The rest of its face resembled a bloody, broken boxer after a knockout. It made Mrs. Bates from PSYCHO look like a beauty queen. I let out a subdued yelp, whereupon I detected uncontrolled laughter from the living room.

My cousin walked in, pulled back the covers on my bed and introduced me to BEULAH, a department store mannequin of ill repute. My mother being awakened by my scream came in holding her hand over her heart inquiring as to the apparent distress taking place in her house.

After all parties had calmed down, I once again reflected on the meaning of this moment. Knowing that I had resolved to enter a parallel universe of normalcy that football-throwing night on the bridge, I began to wonder if indeed I would ever be granted the serenity of a peaceful existence. Should I let this latest debacle of genetic witchery go unanswered? Should I pass it off as another meaningless act of family humor? Could I be strong and true to my convictions? No, I had to get even. Maybe I had just one more act of vengeance left in me.

Having laid Beulah on the living room carpet with all concerned gathered about, I began to devise my plans. The only person still unaware of these events was my dad, who could sleep through an atomic blast. Realizing that he was the one who brought this comic cousin into my midst, he was therefore the one ultimately responsible for my current state of stress. I vowed to turn the tide and pull one on him. I engaged the assistance of my mom and outlined my scheme.

The following morning, as my dad arose from bed, my mom, in a sorrowful manner, approached my dad, telling him that I had run over and killed a girl on the way home from work the previous night, and not knowing what to do, and not wanting to involve the police, had brought her home and put her into the back yard hammock. He quickly dressed, and went outside, proceeded to cuddle up with Beulah, and placing his arm around her, calmly lit a cigarette. He was in on it from the beginning. I had been had again for the second time in eight hours.

We all had fun with Beulah that summer. We put her in the garbage can with an arm sticking out and watched the reaction of the garbage man which was rather disappointing, as he merely left her lying in the driveway. I caught a lot of attention driving to the lake in my corvette convertible, top down with Beulah in the front seat. I left her on the beach on a blanket one day and enjoyed a wide array of screams and reactions. I wondered what that retired FBI agent would have said about that one.

I hoped that with that latest episode, the Walton practical joke gene had run its course, surely, Beulah was the grand finale. I was wrong again. Another theatrical performance of unbridled audacity, which would go down as the all time family classic, occurred at the 1972 U.S. Open at Pebble Beach, California

My older brother Bob and I each took some leave from the Air Force to attend the 1972 U.S. Open. He brought his wife and two sons and we had tickets for the final two days.

That golf tournament was memorable for me for three reasons. It was the tournament where Jack Nicklaus hit his famous one iron shot

Center Dock

on hole 17 which hit the flagstick and dropped two inches from the hole; it was where I discovered Irish coffee and it was where I became a participant in one of the most bizarre and insane acts ever conceived by mankind.

This time my older brother was the instigator. I was dragged into it at the last moment. Unknown to me, he had a putter inside his pant leg when we entered the course. His older son Robin was wearing a jump suit not too unlike the garb worn by caddies at that time. Just behind the first tee at Pebble Beach is the practice putting green where the pros hone their putting skills just prior to teeing off.

After entering the course behind the pro shop, my brother and his son excused themselves, and told us to wait for them by the practice green. A few minutes later, much to my horror, my brother and his son walked from the pro staging area decked out in full golf attire including towels, balls and visors, onto the practice green, whereupon, three balls are dropped by the "caddie," and the "pro" began putting. This outrageous act went on for about two minutes when suddenly, his wife approached him requesting his autograph. A few minutes later, his other son approached also requesting an autograph. Oh my God! Knowing that this caper would probably go down as one of the all time family classics, I had to become part of it. I walked out and requested an autograph. A small crowd began to gather. I thought we were going, to be arrested any moment. I was nearly hysterical, when two old ladies, strangers, also approached requesting autographs. That was it. I slowly meandered into the pro shop knowing that possibly our military careers would end and we would be spending several days in jail. As quickly as it began, it ended. All parties departed the area. I followed them back to our car, where all evidence of the act was deposited. We spent two uneventful days watching Nicklaus win another Open and drinking Irish coffee.

I've thought of this incident many times over the years, and have failed to ascertain its underlying meaning. It has left an indelible mark on my psyche. I keep asking myself if it really occurred, if it wasn't just a fantasy, or some sort of weird dream. No, it did happen, and we did get by with it. As I get older, I keep trying to understand the significance of that day. Was there a message? Was I missing something? Were these events an omen of pending disaster. I began to wonder if maybe I had been adopted. Then one day, I was enlightened by a dramatic thought.

Was there a connection between these events and my love for those days at the lake? Perhaps the lake provided a sanctuary from these genetic outbursts. Perhaps the lake represented a more normal and understandable lifestyle. Perhaps the lake established the framework for my future, without the burden of practical jokes and acts of insanity. Perhaps it was my refuge from the world.

What was wrong with my family? Why do we do these things? Is it not possible to control the DNA structure which causes this kind of behavior? I continue to recognize the effect of this gene today in my children and my grandchildren. What comes next? Which one will do it? That question was recently answered at a Scottsdale Arizona restaurant where my grandson Brady, who at thirteen months, recently divulged his propensity for Walton cornasity.

Just after we were seated, little Brady looked up at the ceiling, and soon we were all looking up, whereupon he points at everyone and giggles-we had been had. The gene lives. This same stunt was often pulled by my dad on my mom. Unbelievable! God help us!

Charade Lady

BIKINI-CLAD GIRLS added spice to the sometimes monotonous times at the lake. They were in abundance, all shapes, sizes, and age groups. They were all beautiful. If Playboy magazine had wanted to do a spread on the "Girls of Pfafflin Lake," they would have had no trouble finding more than ample talent.

We had what we referred to as the "Bobsy Twins." These were two late teen Newburgh dolls who were just stunning. They both had wonderful outgoing personalities, good manners, and demeanors that would rival any super model.

Another frequent beach queen, also from Newburgh, captivated the beach with her beauty and lovely smile. I was uncertain as to her age, but for some reason I sensed a mysterious and sinister force surrounding her. She appeared distant and aloof and more often than not would spend the entire day on the beach just sitting alone. I tagged her as a potential evaluator. My suspicions would be proven correct four years later.

In 1967, I was assigned to an Air Force unit at Fort Lee, Virginia. One day we had a tour come through, and one of the folks recognized me and told me he was from Newburgh. We got to talking about everyone we knew, and the subject of this particular young lady came up. He told me that she was attending college in Richmond, Virginia, just a few miles up the road. I was elated.

After several attempts dealing with campus operators, I managed to find her dormitory phone number. She was glad to hear from me, and we exchanged the usual pleasantries. At this point, I wish to point out that I had no romantic interest in this girl whatsoever. I merely wanted to talk about old times, even though they were not that old, and ascertain the whereabouts of some of the old gang. I invited her to dinner, and we had a scrumptious meal at the Fort Lee Officers' Club, followed by a brief tour of the giant radar command and control facility where I worked.

All the way back to Richmond, we talked about our experiences at the lake, her college, and the Vietnam War. It had been a fun evening, until just about three blocks from her dorm, when she turned to me and confirmed my earlier suspicions in a most dramatic way. At that time, I was driving a 1965 white Corvette convertible. That evening I was wearing an old brown suede jacket.

I experienced that night something that forever changed my view of women. After that night I became so distrustful and disgusted with women that it affected me the remainder of my life. She got real close to my face and told me that she was not impressed with either my car or my suede jacket, and that she was certain I was trying to impress and manipulate her, but failing miserably. She then called me a clod and said that this encounter had been a total charade, and she never intended to see me again.

What had I done to bring this on? Perhaps I had inadvertently farted or blown a booger into her hair. In either case, I was hurt to the core and in many ways never recovered. Never before or since had I ever witnessed such an act of arrogance and insensibility than that night. I assume she totally misunderstood my intentions and may have thought that an intimate encounter was about to be suggested, which it was not.

As previously mentioned, I just wanted to say hello and share our common experiences from the lake. For the next week I carefully went over every detail of that night and finally hit upon a possible explanation. Perhaps she had become an anti-war radical , and I had represented a symbol of her hatred toward the military. Maybe I really was a clod.

There was one redeeming aspect gained from this experience. I knew that my ability to spot evaluators and manipulators was reaffirmed. That skill has never failed me, even to this day.

My most memorable experience with the opposite sex that fourth summer was the day my then girlfriend Karen B. and two of her friends showed up at the lake, and graced the premises with their lovely legs. All three of these creatures were famous for their long legs and related anatomical characteristics.

As I sat on the center dock, all three glided smoothly, like goddesses, through the water toward me. Never before had I experienced such rapture and awe. With their long blond hair gracefully following in their wake, each approached the dock, and like devil-blessed temptresses, climbed the ladder and entered into my world. For the next twenty minutes I was captivated, teased, and charmed to unbelievable heights. What had I done to deserve this? It was another reckoning. My attitude toward women was improving. I had been dating Karen for most of that summer and was glad to see her at the lake. We got along perfectly. Her brother and I had played football against each other in High school. She was my soul mate, and my parents loved her dearly. However, we soon drifted apart as she found other romantic interests in college. She was also concerned that our religious faiths were different. Apparently, that fact had significance with her mother.

That winter, and just a few weeks before Christmas, I began dating Carolyn M., an AOPI (Alpha Omicron PI). She was a darling little black-haired beauty. She was to my delight, and a non-evaluator. She didn't have to be, her parents did it for her. One night at her parents' home I was drilled as to what courses I took in high school all the way through my current year in college. They tried to ascertain some personal data on my parents plus a host of other related subjects. They even asked me what my most challenging experience had been. I started to tell them it was trying to date your daughter; instead I sort of put a halt to the twenty question game by answering that it had been my attempt to avoid bee stings at the lake. I will never know if I passed their muster.

Carolyn M and I became an item, but not for long. For some reason, she asked another guy to her sorority's holiday formal. I believe it may have been brought on by outside influences. In any case things began to deteriorate and the calm was replaced by stress.

I didn't feel too bad, because in late December I began dating the former Miss Evansville. This highly enraged Carolyn M, and our relationship began to crumble and eventually died out.

My Miss Evansville lady surprised me after about three weeks by telling me she had throat cancer and would be leaving school. I felt bad for her and her family. I was once again unattached and turned toward my studies in an attempt to raise my grades. I was having difficulty reading by then due to my deteriorating eyesight.

I believe it was about the middle of January when I met Brenda R. I don't recall how I met her, but I was in need of a soul mate to keep me warm. We quickly developed a strong attachment toward each other, although deep down, I felt as if we actually couldn't stand each other. I pinned her in early February. This meant that she wore my fraternity pin as a jester of good faith and other associated romantic mush. That same month, I again tasted lake water.

It was a common practice with our fraternity, as with most other fraternities, to toss all newly-pinned brothers into a lake. One never knew when it was coming. For me and another poor soul, our time came on one of the coldest February nights of the year. Following a typical boring fraternity meeting, we were both grabbed, tied up, gagged and placed under a blanket in the rear of a pick-up truck .

We were then driven several blocks to a lake on the grounds of the Evansville State Hospital whereupon we were untied and without fanfare or hesitation systematically tossed through an inch of ice into the freezing water. I knew then that whatever sex life I may have had coming in the future was gone forever. That water was so cold, I was certain that I had left parts of my anatomy in that lake.

It was also a tradition to serenade the girl at her residence following the dunking. Since Brenda was residing in the girls dorm at the college, we all gathered outside her room and at 12:30 at night with me wrapped in blankets; our fraternity serenaded Brenda along with at least a hundred others hanging out of their windows. If that wasn't enough, we then all went to Art and Helen's Bar and ingested a few brews. God-what a night.

Well, needless to say, my parents were concerned about the seriousness of my new relationship. They didn't view Brenda's assertiveness with approving eyes and proceeded to make my life semi-miserable. As it turned out, their concerns were in vain, due to a discovery I made one night. It seemed Miss Brenda was seeing other guys behind my back. I thought about getting a dog.

End of an Era

THE END CAME at the close of the 1967 season, when the lake closed its doors to all recreational activity for good. At that time, I had graduated from college and was serving in the military. My brother wrote me telling me of the closure. I was saddened yet relieved that the Pfafflin family had been released from their burden. I was certain control of the environment at the lake had become nearly impossible.

The times were quite different now for all of us. The strong disciplined family value system of the pre and post World War II era was crumbling. Violence was increasing, institutions were distrusted, leaders challenged and the nation's youth, disillusioned about society were becoming confused and hostile. Kennedy was dead, his brother Bobby, and Martin Luther King soon would be, and the nation was mired in Vietnam.

When I learned of the closing, It felt as though a part of me had died, or at least been unfairly taken away. This place had constituted a major part of my childhood, and would forever impact my life. The memories, the events, the laughter, and most of all the people will forever be a part of me. It seemed that time, beer hill, and I'm sure the ever increasing cost of liability insurance contributed to the decision. It was time for the Pfafflin family to recover and retire to a less stressful life style.

Center Dock

I had accumulated a total of 96 saves over those years, most of which were NYF kiddy saves, but nevertheless, I was proud of all of them. Mr. Pfafflin continued to run his dogs, clear brush, and work the property. I learned later that year that he was contemplating selling the property to a developer. That meant homes. Why not? I could not think of a better place to live. I vowed then that beer hill would someday be my living room.

I made it a point to visit the Pfafflin family whenever I was home on leave. I don't remember the year, but the lake property had indeed been sold, and development had begun. Mr. and Mrs. Pfafflin had built a new home a bit further away from the lake on Outer Grey Road where they spent their remaining days.

The last time I saw Mr. Pfafflin, he was a stooped and fragile looking man. I was told that Mrs. Pfafflin passed away that year. Mr. Pfafflin no longer recognized me. I knew I would never see him again.

I wanted to someday live at the lake, and while still in the Air Force, I continued to formulate a strategy which would allow me to once again traverse its grounds. Many years later, following my military retirement, my wife and I looked at a few available homes on the Lake and came close to making an offer on one. However, like every utensil dropped on the floor from the dinner table, it was barely out of reach. Following my Air Force retirement, I accepted a job teaching college accounting in Owensboro Kentucky. I often drove around the lake whenever in the area and continue to marvel at its beauty and peaceful setting. I lost track of the remaining Pfafflin family, although I still believe that Ron Pfafflin, a nephew, still lives on the property.

Gone now is the old Pfafflin residence where I spent many hours and ate many homemade cookies. Gone is all evidence of past adventures and endeavors. Gone are the docks, the scenes of so much drama. Gone is a part of many people's youth. All that remains are the remnants of a landscape dotted with upscale homes.

The closing of the lake, to me, symbolized the end of an era, especially for the little kids. Gone were the days of cowboys and Indians, climbing trees, catching lightning bugs, playing hide and seek, and struggling to make it to the center dock. Their world would be surrounded by guns, violence, media and internet garbage. It seems they would be denied the right to be kids. They would be pushed into adulthood too soon without ever experiencing grass between their toes, mud-pies, tea parties, the smell of a country lake, or what it means to stay out in the rain. The lake represented the last vestiges of youthful innocence.

Those days at the lake had changed me. I started working there as a naïve, shy, pious city kid, and emerged as a modern day Huckleberry Finn. I still am.

We now live in an over complex society, characterized by big houses, fancy cars, computers, an unquenchable thirst for wealth, and career accomplishment at all costs. I would trade all of that in an instant for just one more dash across the lake, one more leap off the twenty-seven footer, and one more hour in the chair on the center dock.

Carl Pfafflin passed away in 1969.

About the Author

Steve Walton resides in Phoenix, Arizona along with his two children and two grandchildren. His wife of 38 years is deceased. He is currently working on his next book ***The Mushrooms,*** which relates his experiences as an Air Force Radar Weapons Control Officer. He continues to swim everyday and still clings to the hope of someday living at Pfafflin Lake.

Aqua
~~OTC~~ 4
Hydro Cortizn
     cream
Anti Itch -
  Kristen